JOY IN YOUR GARDEN

A SEASONAL GUIDE TO GARDENING

JOY IN YOUR GARDEN

A SEASONAL GUIDE TO GARDENING

JOY BOSSI & KAREN BASTOW

CFI
SPRINGVILLE, UTAH

ISBN 13: 978-1-59955-290-3

Published by CFI, an imprint of Cedar Fort, Inc., 2373 W. 700 S., Springville, UT 84663
Distributed by Cedar Fort, Inc. www.cedarfort.com

LIBRARY OF CONGRESS CATALOGING-IN-PUBLICATION DATA

Bossi, Joy, 1948-
  Joy in your garden : a seasonal guide to gardening / Joy Bossi and Karen
Bastow.
      p. cm.
  ISBN 978-1-59955-290-3 (acid-free paper)
  1. Gardening. I. Bastow, Karen, 1953- II. Title.

  SB450.97.B67 2010
  635--dc22

            2009017318

Cover and page design by Angela D. Olsen
Cover design © 2010 by Lyle Mortimer
Edited by Melissa Caldwell

Printed in China

10 9 8 7 6 5 4 3 2 1

Printed on acid-free paper

JOY'S DEDICATION

To Dr. Seville Flowers, a short giant of a man who truly loved teaching,
and with contagious delight, introduced me to the wonder of plants.

And to my grandson, Linus, to remind him that
Grandma Joy will always be in his garden.

KAREN'S DEDICATION

To my grandfather, Ross Dickson, who shared with me his love of gardening
and didn't mind when I planted gladioli bulbs upside down. He was everything a grandpa
and a gardener should be—growing not only plants but a granddaughter
who will treasure his memory forever.

JOY'S ACKNOWLEDGMENTS

Because so many people, especially my dear dad, wondered when in the world
I was going to write a book, this did come to pass. Thank you, dear friends, for
continuing to encourage me and push just a little to finally get my
voice translated into the written word.

KAREN'S ACKNOWLEDGMENTS

With gratitude to my loving and very patient husband, Steve,
and youngest daughters Kirsten, Kaylee, and Kaitlynn for taking over
while I spent many hours at the computer and in the garden.

To my older children, Bryan and Emily; Kristina; and Nathan and Spring,
for their encouragement, love, and support.

And to three wonderful grandsons, Brock, Zachary, and Luke—the newest generation
of gardeners in our family—thanks for the hugs and the laughter.

AND TOGETHER, JOY AND KAREN ACKNOWLEDGE

Pat and Tom Westaway, for their unwavering support and encouragement.
Annette Boren, for going above and beyond the call of cheerleader.

TABLE OF CONTENTS

Preface
xi

The Garden

SEPTEMBER, OCTOBER, AND NOVEMBER

CONTENTS

PREFACE

This is a book for all garden lovers—even those who haven't yet had a garden or those who have been working in their garden, but it isn't all they thought it was going to be. This is a book for those who may have once, long ago, toiled in a garden but who can only remember the toiling part—perhaps weeding was all they *did* in the garden. This is a book for those who would just like a few tips and suggestions for getting the very most out of their garden plot.

Joy in the Garden is the name of my radio program. For fifteen years I have had the pleasure of greeting Saturday morning with thousands of my good gardening buddies in conversation. As some things just seem to blend into one another, my transition from television gardening spots to a radio program to a consulting business to more television segments winds like a path through a garden. Sometimes there were unexpected turns, followed by incredibly beautiful vistas. Occasionally, weeds seemed to grow over everything I planted. But serendipity was the winner in the end—or beginning, really.

Marriage and two wonderful children followed a degree in botany. During my college years, I put myself through the last three years of school teaching botany classes and labs at Brigham Young University in Provo, Utah. Changes in my life led to adventures in substitute teaching, emergency preparedness, and gifted education. When a chance to return to botany through working in a garden center presented itself, I jumped on it. A wonderful family-owned nursery and landscape business was hiring and that—that has made all the difference. While working for Redwood Nursery and Landscaping in Salt Lake City, I passed a rigorous three-part test and became a Certified Nurseryman. Since that is no longer a politically correct designation, I carry the title of Certified Nursery Professional. It is my honor to be associated with the good folk of the UNLA—Utah Nursery and Landscape Association. During my time at the nursery, I also completed the Master Gardener course through the Utah State Extension Office in Salt Lake County, Utah. Between the two organizations I figure I know, or have rubbed shovels with, most of the best, most knowledgeable, and generous gardeners found anywhere.

I do enjoy speaking fluent "plant" with the professionals, flinging about the botanical names with shameless abandon. But I love speaking "pigeon" plant even more. That is probably because I tend to make up my own gardening words that don't appear in any botanical, horticultural, or gardening written material. The written word just doesn't convey my wild gestures and pointing, so we have included a list of "Joy-isms" to help you visualize some of my words and phrases.

While at Redwood Nursery I taught classes and started doing consultations for some of our customers. When Rebecca Reheis (now Rebecca Kohl of Rebecca's Garden in Minneapolis) started doing gardening segments in conjunction with her weather reports on a local television station, Redwood Nursery built a demonstration garden near the station's parking lot. I was asked to go "on camera" to give some information about trees during a broadcast she did from our nursery. Wow! That wasn't scary—it was fun! One segment led to another and I was asked to take over her gardening spot when she moved. The radio program came into being because a sponsor wanted to have a Saturday morning radio show with a call-in format. Well, how about that! Because my sweet little mom had been recording my TV spots,

I just happened to have an audition tape all ready to go. *Joy in the Garden* started in September of 1994. Of course, serendipity couldn't leave things alone, and so the radio program was the connection to a local TV program, *Good Things Utah* and that about completed the circle. My day job, though, is as a garden consultant. The truth is that I really consider myself a Gardening Cheerleader.

Karen Bastow and I met while we were each doing some independent contractor work for the Square Foot Gardening Foundation. Here is her gardening story:

Some of the earliest memories I have are of following my grandpa around in his garden while he lovingly called me his "Best Helper Girl." I became his shadow as we completed every garden task together. Spring was always exciting when Grandpa hitched up a borrowed horse to a harrow. He would put me on top of the horse, and we would circle the large garden plot, waking up the soil from its winter sleep. After raking and smoothing, it was time to begin planting. Long stakes with twine guided the hoe as Grandpa deftly carved out a straight row. As soon as I was strong enough, I became his "Best Water Girl," and after filling an old metal watering can, I walked up and down the rows pouring out the life-giving water. Side by side, Grandpa and I knelt in the soft soil and carefully planted each seed, watching with anticipation in the following days for the first tip of green to poke its head above ground. To this day, the old watering can sits in a place of honor in my home as a symbol of the love of a grandpa who taught a granddaughter that most of life's lessons can be learned in a garden.

The day of our irrigation turn was always exciting; the streams of water flowed down each furrow just inviting little feet to jump in and squish in the mud. And the harvest—well there is just nothing like eating peas fresh from the garden; or pulling a carrot, rinsing it off with the hose, and hearing that crunch of goodness; or the indescribable sweetness of a plump sun-warmed raspberry. Grandpa always entered his produce in the County Fair in Morgan, Utah, and again, I was by his side readying the displays. He always made me feel that the blue ribbons were my doing.

Is it any wonder that my love of gardening has continued throughout my life? My husband and I have tried to instill this same love of gardening into each of our six children. Gardening has always been for me the very best of hobbies, and it is only in the last few years that it has become my part-time profession as well. During these years, I have enjoyed writing and speaking about gardening. An interesting twist was having my garden filmed by BYU-TV for an episode of *Homegrown* showing how to do Square Foot Gardening. Some of the most heartwarming gardening experience of my life are the opportunities to take my love of gardening and participate in humanitarian project in Kenya showing people who are desperately in need how to garden.

Like Joy, I am a Master Gardener through the Utah State Extension Office, except I took my course in Weber County, Utah. Gardeners are a wonderful group of people to have as your mentors, teachers, and friends. As your enthusiasm starts bubbling, I recommend that you find your local Master Gardener Association and learn about their organization.

This book is a result of our mutual desire to guide people on their journey through their own garden. Karen and I are convinced that once you find something productive, therapeutic, healthy, and delightful, you really ought to share it with everybody! And because we kept thinking of handy-dandy ideas that didn't quite fit in the flow of the book, we decided to add the Bonus Boxes . . . then when even more ideas came to mind, we threw in a couple of *Extra* Bonus Boxes! We hope you'll enjoy the sometimes quirky information.

Also, because Karen lives at a higher mountain altitude and has a very short growing season, we've included some "High on a Mountain Tips" for those of you who live in similar locations. These tips will help you extend the season long enough to get the harvest you desire.

Everyone deserves to experience the connection to green growing things. "Hug a tree" is a better prescription than you may realize. Trees give us more than just oxygen, though that is life-giving enough. Cooling our environment, cleansing the air, and providing food and shelter are also gifts from our gentle green friends. Gardening in any form *is* a therapeutic endeavor. Do you want the stress and pain of your life to diminish? Poke around in the soil for a while. No garden near you to call your own? Buy a potted geranium or a miniature lemon tree. Water, fertilize, prune, inhale the fragrance, let the flowers dazzle you, and you will start to know peace.

Whether you are fortunate enough to own or rent the back forty acres or only have permission to garden in the front ten square feet at your apartment, you, my friend, are a gardener! We believe everyone can have success in their garden—you only need to grasp a few correct principles, and then you can govern your growing space with confidence. That is what this book is about. Karen and I believe in YOU and YOUR garden. We want to share information that

will connect you with the garden life around you. We believe that growing flowers, trees, fruit, vegetables, and even the lawn can bring a kind of satisfaction and serenity into your life that can't be found any other way. Is it safer to grow your own produce? Can you say "salmonella" and "E-coli?" Is produce from your backyard garden really better than store bought? Have you *tasted* a garden-ripened tomato? If not, it's about time you did! Even carrots and potatoes have the store variety beat hands down in the taste department. And we haven't even mentioned peaches, peppers, or pumpkins!

Starting this book with gardening in September is to get you thinking about *what* you do in your garden, *when* you do the things you do, and more important, *why* you do those things! The information in this book is directed at newbie gardeners, returning gardeners, and those gardeners who enjoy a good chuckle while expanding their gardening vision. Just because the beginning section starts with September, however, doesn't mean you must start reading there. If you just got this book and it's March, you may want to jump right to the March-April-May section and dig (every pun intended) right in!

We offer this book to you, our gardening friends—those of you we have known for years, and those of you we have yet to meet. You can do it! This will be the best year in your garden (or pot of petunias) ever. It may be just the beginning or a return to the soil, but a garden is a thing of beauty and a joy forever—so get out there and find joy in YOUR garden!

In The Beginning

JUST WHAT IS A GROWING SEASON?

Have you ever wondered exactly what constitutes a growing season? If a plant goes in the ground on a Tuesday and is dead by Saturday, would the growing season be only four days long?

Spring is the starting gun for some growing seasons. The sun comes out, the snow melts, and folks are off to the garden with a trowel in hand. Yes siree! Spring through fall—now that's a growing season.

Gardening in the southern United States demands a different definition for a growing season. And the growing season in upstate Vermont is still another kettle of tomatoes! Even if gardens are at the same latitude, altitude will shift the length of the growing season. Unless you are stuck in the year-round gardening pattern, you need to know when the last killing frost strikes in the spring, and then you need to know the date of the first killing frost in the fall. The days in between—that's your growing season. Weathermen keep track of these sort of things, and you can look up the specific dates for this on your friendly, neighborhood computer. Weathermen will give you a date that is the average of all recorded first and last frosts.

The date of the average *last* frost can be a signal to start the growing season and plant, plant, plant. However, in a garden without protection, a later-than-average spring frost can kill off all of those tender plants, and you'll find yourself replanting, replanting, replanting. Counting on a long growing season, right up to the date of the average last frost will sometimes end up leaving you with green, never-to-ripen produce. Just remember: "average" is somewhere between so cold the plants freeze and good growing weather.

That same "average" can give you an extended fall to ensure perfect produce or put ten inches of snow and freezing rain down on the pumpkin patch.

Planning or planting, dreaming or scheming, September *is* such a reassuring time to start the growing season. Even if you are not ready to start planting, you can start growing. Say what? What can you grow without planting? You can grow your soil!

SOIL

So you want a pretty healthy garden, eh? Nothing you plant is going to reach its full healthy productive potential if your soil is weak, sick, or shallow.

Now, soil isn't dirt—no sirree. Dirt is what's left on your car after a particularly short summer rain shower. Dirt is what accumulates in the corner of the garage or is tracked into the house on your feet. Dirt is what often masquerades as soil around a newly built home (especially if the house is the last one to be built in the neighborhood). The dirt you see when the topsoil is scraped from the surface is called subsoil, and even if it's dark brown, it isn't topsoil.

Topsoil is built up over hundreds of years. When there is sufficient rain coupled with plant material that regularly dies or is killed, perhaps by lightening or floods, the combination can result in topsoil. With enough water, mineral-rich plant material, and living organisms both large and small, you get dark, rich topsoil is formed. Beneath the topsoil, subsoil is found. Subsoil is the original mineral "dirt" deposited by forces of geology—or perhaps was brought in as fill dirt to raise the level of a low area. Topsoil is a fragile commodity. Wind can blow it away, people can haul it away, and even a flood can wash it away in a matter of minutes. Nature "grows" topsoil in proportion to the amount of plant and animal remains that receive natural precipitation.

Soil is an accumulation of living organisms, their remains and residue, and mineral particles. It is what accounts for the tastiest tomatoes, the largest dahlias, the most flavorful basil, and the greenest lawn in the entire neighborhood.

Soil consists of four primary components:

1. Mineral particles
2. Organic material (living and dead)
3. Water
4. Air

Ideal soil contains roughly 40 percent mineral particles, 30 percent air spaces and water combined, and 3–10 percent organic matter. (Sigh—were it ever so.) If the organic portions hit 5 percent in the Rocky Mountain area we are thrilled with our wonderful soil. Truthfully, it is more often 1–2 percent leaving the gardener with way more top dirt than top soil.

TESTING THE SOIL

To give you a rough idea of how much of each kind of particle you have in your garden soil, perform the following test:

- Take either a pint or quart glass jar.
- Fill the jar about ⅔ with clean water.
- Scoop about a cup of your soil into the jar.
- Screw on a tight lid.
- Shake vigorously until the soil is all mixed in the water.
- Place the jar safely where it won't be mistaken for something else (I don't know *what* else, but if you have kids . . .)
- Let it rest and settle overnight.

After it settles, you will find layers that tell the story of your soil. At the bottom of the jar will be the larger and heavier sand and pebble particles. Next, you'll find the smaller silt particles, topped by the clay layer. If organic matter has been added to your soil, a fourth layer, because it is the lightest, will be at the top. Some of the organic pieces such as wood, may even still be suspended in or floating on the top of the water. Unless you took the sample from somewhere like Iowa or Ohio, the bottom mineral layers will usually be far larger than the top organic layer.

To help appreciate the soil beneath your feet, take a moment to understand the characteristics of the soil texture. Sand is coarse, feels gritty, does not store many nutrients, and does not retain or take up water well. Clay, on the other hand, feels sticky and slick, has a high storage of nutrients, and holds and takes up water. Silt sits right in the middle of the two, is smooth when dry, and takes up and holds a moderate amount of water and nutrients. Most soil is a combination of these three particles. The movement of air, water, and roots through the soil is affected by the soil texture and structure.

The percent associated with each layer in your jar will help you determine the composition of your soil. For example, if a soil is composed of ⅓ clay, ⅓ silt and ⅓ sand, it is called loam. Loam is the texture that is best for plant growth. If clay makes up more than ⅓ of the loam, the soil is a "clay loam." More than ⅓ sand and it's called "sandy loam."

The mineral portion of the soil is made of these different-sized particles. The hundreds of miles of rock walls built around early homesteads in the United States stand as examples of the "particles" with sizes roughly matching up with cantaloupes or bed pillows.

CLAY SOIL

Many gardeners struggle with the difficulties created by trying to grow in heavy clay soil.

Tiny clay particles—visible only under a microscope and measuring less than half the diameter of a human hair—create a heavy soil because of the compacted weight and lack of air spaces.

Clay can be a horrible mess in the garden, but it has its advantages. Clay rarely gets the kudos it deserves. As the tiniest soil particle, water and nutrients cling to it better than any other soil type. Watering and fertilizing are needed less often than with the other soil types. Okay, that pretty much ends the advantages. (Unless you count adding a little straw and water, throwing it around for a while, and ending up with adobe an advantage.)

SANDY SOIL

Sandy soil is the never-ending abyss into which water and nutrients are forever pouring. Being the largest of the soil particles, it does allow for perfect drainage. That pretty much ends the advantage to sandy soil except you rarely break the handle of a garden fork while trying to turn the soil.

ROCKY SOIL

Gardeners in rocky soil never need to worry about drainage either—water trickles down between rocks just fine. The difficulty comes in removing the rocks before trying to plant. In cases such as this, the dynamite solution quickly comes to mind—*something drastic* is needed to break the big rocks into little ones! Having sacrificed two fine spading forks and a cast aluminum trowel trying to pry rocks out of my garden, I have been on the brink of the "dynamite solution" several times in the garden. Living within 20 feet of my neighbors and across the street from

Bonus Box: If you should be working in clay soils, here's a tip to keep your shoes or boots relatively clean. When the clay is wet—and it usually is when not giving the clay impression of concrete—the buildup on and around the soles of your shoes can be awful. You can gain a full 10 pounds after working in your garden, and scraping the goop off is bothersome! Try putting plastic newspaper bags over your shoes. Several layers on each foot can be used just like how race horse jockeys use layered goggles. Peel off one at a time when they start collecting several inches of the heavy clay.

the local elementary school, I am forced to forego the KABOOM my rocks so richly deserve.

"GROWING" YOUR SOIL

You know you can grow plants, but did you know that you can also "grow" soil by enhancing it with good organic matter? To create healthy, productive topsoil from soil of any particle size, just add compost! Compost allows sand to hold water and nutrients long enough for roots to absorb them. Compost separates clay particles, so water and air can both be available to the plant. Two opposite problems are solved with the same material—good quality organic matter.

Rocky soil like mine requires continual additional compost but after, oh, twenty years or so, the result is a garden with great soil. Along with adding organic matter, you will also be continually subtracting rocks. A little process called "heaving" brings rocks up to the surface after every winter. No, you're not paranoid—some dastardly person didn't sneak in at night and quietly dump a bucket full of rocks in the very garden bed you cleared out last fall. It was the freeze/thaw cycle of winter, not the neighbor who thought it was payback time for seven bushels of zucchini left on his porch last fall. Constant adding (organic matter) and subtracting (rocks) will result in some mighty fine soil. (At least this is the case in the areas where you have previously and consistently dug holes and planted something.) In the hinterland of my backyard, under the 50-year-old Vinca major vines, lies untouched ground. Not too long ago, I had visions of planting a dwarf peach tree back there. After the first *clank*, I put away the shovel and decided I would find a much better place for the little tree later, on the other side of the garden.

Joy's Saga of the Rocky Soil

I still ache remembering the hole we tried to dig to plant our first peach tree. (And I use the term "we" loosely!) In fact it was the first hole my husband and I dug for any reason on our little suburban lot. Knowing wide was more important than deep, I marked the diameter of the hole to be twice as wide as the pot containing the little peach tree. After only two scoops with the shovel came the *clank*—the unmistakable sound of metal colliding with rock. "Well," thought I, "I'll just dig wider first." With each clank, scuffle, and scritch, I stopped and pried up another rock. Some were softball sized, most tennis ball caliber, and a cantaloupe look-alikes. But by then, the hole was only half as deep as the root ball.

There was a rock right in the middle of the hole that had to go. It looked to be maybe five inches long and about three inches wide. First attempt was the time-honored pry method. But alas, no movement—just the shovel scraping along the edge of the rock. Next I tried digging a moat around the entire rock to see which side was holding up the process. Four inches down the entire circumference of the rock and it was still five inches by three inches in size but now seemed to be about 8 inches deep. Not yet daunted, I put down the shovel and began scooping out dirt with a trowel. I was thinking if I could reach where the bottom of the rock begins curving under I could go back to the pry-it-with-the-shovel method. After the hole was another four inches deep, I had to lie down on my stomach to reach the bottom of the trench for more scoop, CLANK, scoop, CLANK. I thought, "Just a little further and I'll be under the bottom of this stubborn rock." Another four inches came and went with still no bottom curve in sight. By now my husband was wondering out loud if the tree wouldn't do better over on the other side of the garden.

"No!" I hissed between clenched teeth. "This spot is just FINE!"

I figured a few more inches and I'd have it out, but this proved to be an inaccurate estimate. There is now a 5″ x 3″ x 24″ rock that holds a place of honor in the curving rock wall around my back garden. Turns out the rock that taunted me for nearly two hours was lying on its end pointing upwards. But I won!

You would think that removing the rocks from the hole would be the most difficult part of planting a tree in rocky soil. Not so, my gardening friend. Put the tree in the hole and just *try* to find enough soil to back fill it. There were barely two shovels full of soil that came out of the entire hole. It was *all* rocks.

I learned a valuable lesson that day. Soil must be grown or brought in to fill the holes dug in rocky soil. I parleyed the two scoops of soil to fill in the hole by adding superb compost along with the rocks smaller than a ping pong ball and mixing well. At least the little soil between the surrounding rocks vaguely matched the soil in the hole!

COMPACTED SOIL

Soil holds both water and air and they should be in roughly equal portions. Compaction due to construction vehicles can turn dirt into near-concrete heaviness. After the dump trucks, backhoes, and bulldozers leave, the top dirt is usually brought in and spread around. It seems soft enough when you are trying to plant, and you remember to add a few inches of good organic matter. So digging and planting commence. Lurking just a few inches lower, however, is a layer through which neither water nor roots can penetrate. The particles of soil have been so stomped together that even air is pushed out. Lawn is usually the first plant to signal that this might be a problem. When you dig for a tree or large shrub, it becomes obvious that there is something very, very hard a foot or more below the surface. But lawn sometimes gets planted right over the compaction because it is so easy to bring in some dark dirt, spread it like frosting on a cake and put down your lovely green sod. If you plant in the fall, everything looks superb! The next spring your lawn is great. But when the hot months of July and August beat down, the lawn starts drying up. Roots couldn't grow down through the compacted clay and the high temperatures dry out the top layer of soil daily. Even if you water daily there aren't sufficient roots to keep the grass growing well.

You can test for compaction in the top 8 to 10 inches of soil using a clever little technical device called a screwdriver. Just a regular long thin bladed screwdriver pushed into the soil will give you the results. First water the area, then push the blade down—if it is very hard to push down more than 2 or 3 inches, it's an indication of possible compaction problems. Trees, shrubs, flowers, and vegetables will show signs of poor growth in compacted soil as well.

Organic Matter

MINI GLOSSARY

Bark	From trees! Can be shredded, ground, chopped into chunks, small to large, mixed, or partially composted.
Compost	Partially finished product of the composting cycle—might be from manure, leaves, wood chips, weeds, kitchen scraps, vegetable peelings, fruit rinds. Mostly unrecognizable pieces of brown stuff.
Humus	The final stage of the composting process. The material that is richest in nutrients. It consists of dark brown, very small uniform particles that don't resemble any of the beginning material that was composted.
Lime	Short for limestone, used to raise soil pH making the soil more alkaline. Not organic matter, but a soil additive.
Manure	Backend product of living creatures: cows, horses, chickens, bats, earthworms. Guano=Bat poop. Worm poop=castings.
Mulch	A generic term for something used on top of the soil to retain moisture, inhibit weeds, and modify soil temperature; may or may not be organic.
Soil Conditioner	Any one or mixture of some of the above, dug into the soil. Also called soil amendment—check the fine print on the label to determine what's *really* in the bag.
Top Dressing	One of the above used in a one-half to one-inch layer to make garden beds look extra neat and tidy. Like when company is coming, or a reception is going to be held in your backyard.

THE ELUSIVE ELIXIR OF GARDEN DREAMS

Organic matter takes many forms but is always either living or dead organisms or byproducts of those organisms (manure being the most common). The sizes of the pieces of organic matter range from large heavy chunks to tiny microscopic dots.

THE LIVING SOIL

Many living creatures make up the organic part of soil. Earthworms are recognized by most gardeners who have dug in the soil. Other kinds of worms, many too tiny to be seen easily, live in the soil as well. Microscopic bacteria, fungi, animal, and plant creatures are found numbered by the billions per cubic inch in healthy soil. Most of these "wee beasties" occur naturally in the soil and are either beneficial or harmless. Raw organic matter—the stuff that still looks like its original form such as wood chips, banana peels, fresh manure, sawdust—must be broken down to the basic nutrients that roots can absorb into the plants. We call the process of decomposition "composting." It is discussed in greater detail in the appendix.

As noted, much of the "topsoil" in the Intermountain West contains barely 1–2 percent organic

> Example of ingredient lists found on bags of organic matter at local nurseries:
>
> Bag #1 Composted Steer Manure
>
> Bag #2 Redwood Forest Mulch
> Humus
> Mycorrhizae
>
> Bag #3 Forest Humus
> Chicken Manure
> Rice Hulls
> Bat Guano
> Kelp Meal
> Worm Castings
> Mycorrhizae

material. We need to add organic matter, both raw and composted, to the soil constantly. At least we should if we want even a bare minimum of a 5 percent organic portion of our soil. Arid and semi-arid regions of the USA that receive an average annual rainfall total of less than 20 inches a year have very little natural organic soil. It is the higher rainfall totals which enable the natural sources of organic matter and bacteria to work together to form compost-rich topsoil. Leaves, dead brush and trees, animal carcasses both large and small, and plant residue of all kinds are soon turned into the wonderful organic matter gardeners want for their gardens by the naturally-occurring compost cycle. (See page 125.)

ORGANIC MATTER

The natural top soil found in the farmlands and hardwood forests in nearly every other part of the country is not available to us gardeners in the Southwest and Rocky Mountain regions. Eventually, we come to realize that the source of organic matter for gardens in these two regions won't be the prairie that dates back millennia, nor the ancient hardwood forest with a foot of black organic gold moldering near its roots. No! All good organic material in *your* garden must be either grown or hauled in by *you*.

Compost is that cure-all of soil maladies; that "black gold" so desired at the end of the compost rainbow; the stuff that is exactly what the garden doctor calls for. Unfortunately, the beginning of compost is sometimes described or cursed by gardeners as just "old dead leaf stuff" and is raked up and sent away to the landfill.

Resign yourself to learning how to compost (which by the way, is a very useful piece of knowledge) or head on down to your nearest nursery or garden center and hope the availability of a pickup truck coincides with your need to buy organic material in bulk. That happy combination means the folks at the nursery will load the good stuff into the bed of the truck with a front loader. You simply need to spread it around your garden when you get home. Ordinarily, a half-ton truck carries about a half yard of good stuff (it's better when it's dry, so don't go buying the stuff just after a rainstorm), and depending on the suspension, a full-size truck will haul at least a full cubic yard. A cubic yard amounts to a pile of stuff 3 feet tall, 3 feet wide, and 3 feet long. As you haul this black gold from the truck to the garden, do keep in mind that twice the number of trips with a wheelbarrow *half* full is better than half as many trips with a *full* load that results in a visit to the orthopedic doctor.

WHEN TO ADD ORGANIC MATTER

Because good soil is a combination of many living and decomposing things, growing your own organic soil is the best activity you can do to create or improve your garden. Whether mostly mineral, a satisfying loam, or even an artificial organic blend, the repeated addition of nutritious organic matter will make for smiley faces on the gardener and the gardenees!

Here are some of the terrific chores performed by organic matter in your soil:

1. Mineral nutrients essential for plant growth are held and made available to the little roots longer. In sandy soils the nutrients are flushed out of reach of the roots. The clay particles hold on to the nutrients but because of particle size and chemical properties, they don't want to give them up! Rearranging the clay particles and how they clump together allows release and easier absorption for the plant roots.

2. Organic matter buffers the pH measurement of the soil. It tends to bring any soil nearer to a neutral pH. pH is the chemical way to measure whether something is acidic or alkaline. A measurement of 1–6 is on the acid side of neutral. Pure water is 7, or completely neutral. pH numbers 8–14 are considered alkali or basic. Lemon juice is very acidic and ammonia is a strong alkali. Acid soils are sometimes called "sweet" soils and alkaline ones referred to as "sour." Very organic soils found in Oregon, Maine, and Virginia are said to be sweet. The soils in dry or arid climates including soils in most areas along the Wasatch Front are alkaline.

3. Organic matter increases the water-holding capacity of the soil while at the same time allowing for good water drainage through the soil. This eliminates both the 'sandbox syndrome' where all water and fertilizer sinks away before your very eyes and the 20-pound-boot-pain caused by lugging the accumulated clay mud around on the bottom and sides of your gardening shoes.

4. Cultivation in a soil with a good amount of organic matter is easier on the gardener and the garden tools. Much less mechanical working of the soil is needed. Consistent heavy cultivation can destroy some of the soil structure, even with the addition of organic matter. Tractors and heavy tillers create a hard layer of soil just at the point where the bottom of the tines hit the lowest point in the soil. The tilling beats the air out of the soil and pulverizes the soil particles nearly to dust, creating something akin to a layer of cement. It may be easy to cultivate on top but an impenetrable layer lurks 7 or 8 inches down. You can test for the layer by digging down deeply or poking a heavy rod into the soil. The layer must be

cracked to allow water to continue draining through the soil.

Because there is a continual cycle of organic matter gradually breaking down from the original raw material to the final product of humus and its available nutrients, organic matter must be added to the soil over and over again. That wonderful load of perfectly composted horse manure and sawdust bedding that you dumped, spread, and dug in five years ago has long since completed its work and disappeared.

Every season should find you adding some kind of organic matter to your garden. Okay, maybe not in the dead of winter unless, of course, you live in that state of gardening nirvana called "Zone 8 or 9." (Where is nirvana? Just think San Diego or Seattle.) Ah, year-round gardening! Hold on a pea-picking minute, though! That would mean no luxurious down time in December, January, and February. Planning, not planting, is the supreme gardening pleasure during the winter months. There would be no time for studying the catalogs containing the wonders of the vegetable kingdom—

> **Bonus Box:** When you cover your soil with 2+ inches of good compost, every time it rains or you irrigate, a mild "compost tea" is produced. From the plant roots to the microbes, that tea will make every soil body happy!

new varieties, old favorites, purple cauliflower, flowers that smell like chocolate—the possibilities are endless! Of course, there's not much dreaming time in Zone 8 because you are still out in the garden every waking moment. Yes, well, Zone 5 sounds better to me all the time. To find out which Zone you are gardening in, check out the map on page 139. But I'm getting ahead of myself here.

Since enriching the soil is an all-season gardening task, you don't have to wait until fall garden clean-up time to dig in the organic matter. Nor do you have to bide your time until the soil warms up in the spring. Fall *and* spring seasons are good for the process of adding organic matter. Every time a plant goes in or comes out of your garden is a good time, too. Maybe your garden consists of mostly perennials and none are in need of dividing right away so there is no need to work the soil at all. Not to worry! Spread a two- to three-inch layer of the very best compost over all of the garden beds and it will do wonders for the soil. The worms and other garden helpers in the soil will work on the organic matter and do the micro-tilling for you.

When you've made a good start at growing your soil, whether from naked dirt or wannabe soil, or pretty darn good stuff, it's time to tackle the real point of all this industrious growing—finding joy in your garden!

We've added a few of the "details" that will be helpful as you head to the garden or garden-to-be. Knowledge of the weather, needed tools, and where to find seeds and plants might determine how soon and how well the garden begins to take shape. This useful information is tucked in the back of this book. Commit to memory all these things . . . just kidding! But this reference material will be useful somewhere along your journey to *the garden.*

THE GARDEN

September, October, and November

SEPTEMBER, OCTOBER, AND NOVEMBER

MINI GLOSSARY

Broadleaf evergreen	Shrub or tree that keeps its leaves through the winter, but the leaves aren't needle-like.
Cutting garden	Flowers grown in an area specifically to cut and put in a bouquet.
Deciduous	Plants that lose their leaves during the cold season and get them back in the growing season.
Drip line	An imaginary line drawn on the ground around the tree, under the outer-most branches.
Evergreen	Plants that maintain their green leaves year round.
Flush of blooms	Period of time when the majority of the flowers on a plant are blooming at once.
Fruit	The mature part of a flower that has seeds plus any other part of the plant associated with the seed.
Herbaceous	A plant without any woody tissue.
Green Bin	Recycle container made available by some municipalities.
Microclimate	The climate of a confined space or small geographic area.
Ornamentals	A plant grown for beauty rather than for food.
Pasty (*pas tee*)	[P*a* (as in h*a*t) sty (Not to be confused with P*a* (as in *a*pe) sty.] The traditional Cornish pasty is a baked turnover filled with diced meat, sliced potato and onion.
Saffron crocus	Small, lavender fall-blooming flower; source of the spice saffron.
Tamp	To pack or push something down, especially by tapping repeatedly.

MUSINGS

I've spent well over half of my life bracing for September and the start of the new school year. My "New Year's Eve" was everyone else's Labor Day weekend. For me, that was when new resolutions were made, new classes were started, new clothes and shoes were purchased, along with a family party in the canyon that began with potato salad and chicken and ended with scorched marshmallows. It occurs to me that my yearly gardening adventure always began then, too. That's when temperatures finally cooled enough to spend wonderful mornings and evenings out in the garden.

September is the beginning of the growing season in my garden. It may be a quirky view of the growing season but it gives me a chance (while juice from a homegrown peach or tomato is still dripping off my chin) to dream and scheme about next year's garden. Now is the chance to do what gardeners do best—envision *next* year's successful garden. This is a time to take stock of what died, what nearly died, what should have died, and what ripened, fell, and became bird treats while the gardeners were on vacation.

Listing and eating your successes is heady stuff in the fall. Pick a golden cherry tomato and make a note that you really, really like the Sun Sugar variety of tomato. After slicing a magnificent big tomato for a BLT, you find Big Beef is another favorite to be repeated next year. Pull carrots and onions, dig potatoes for a hearty soup, and make note for next year to plant more onions and carrots.

Take a deep sniff of the flower on the Double Delight rose and be ever so glad someone suggested that variety. Stop harvesting veggies long enough to admire the Saffron crocus appearing like amethyst jewels with tiny crowns of gold in the center all along the driveway.

While basking in the success of ripe tomatoes, excess squash, and gorgeous ornamental grasses, September gives you a chance to seek out sources for new varieties, find helpful answers to puzzling problems, and plan (maybe even on paper) what your dream garden of next year will be. Gaze wistfully at the blazing red maples on the hillside and begin to imagine that same color in your garden next fall. Think to yourself, "Let's see, maybe right over there just past the edge of the lawn in the ground-cover—the Big Tooth Maple should just fit if I move the rhubarb to the other corner!" Then, since fall is for planting, head to the local nursery and look for that one maple left to take home to join your happy garden throng and improve that corner of the garden.

Fall means the flaming-red maple trees are competing with the banana-yellow ash trees for color king of the day. I love the herb Sweet Annie standing tall enough to look me right in the eye. Then, there are the green little baby lemons on the Meyer lemon tree, swelling just large enough to hint at the harvest that will come after the tee comes inside for the winter.

For those folks who must be content to *only* dream because there is not yet a garden to work in, just think, everything will be an improvement from this point on! Just digging in and turning over the soil brightens the future. With plans in hand, the empty stretch of dirt from fence to fence doesn't seem quite so overwhelming. There is hope at the end of the shovel! Gardeners with fully-planted gardens hold on to the same hope—next year the garden will be prettier, neater, and more productive. Now is the time to plan for more beets, enlarge the cutting garden (maybe figure out just what *is* a cutting garden), work to get the lawn greener, perhaps decide where the lawn will be . . . you get the picture.

If the soul longing to dig decides planting is more important than planning, just sticking plants "willey nilley" into the ground will ultimately lead to disappointment: "Oh, it's so pretty—let's buy three and put them along the fence to cover all that white vinyl." Only all three burn to a crisp one month into the next summer because it turns out they needed shade and not a southern exposure against the vinyl fence. See? A few moments of planning and learning can prevent this sort of disaster.

Should it be your lot (tee hee) to face that overwhelming emptiness that is a new home's garden, start by measuring the dimensions of your entire lot. It will make decisions easier if you also jot down lists of "Wouldn't we love . . ." and lists of "We surely don't want . . ."

Just a few details to consider:

- Trees grow best if they are NOT planted in the lawn.
- A tree on the south and/or west side of the property will eventually provide afternoon shade.
- A tree on the east side only casts morning shade.
- A tree on the north gives your *neighbor* afternoon shade.
- Vegetable gardens need as much sun as possible.
- Shrubs and flowers should be planted at least three feet from the foundation of the house.
- Flower, shrub or vegetable gardens DON'T have to run parallel to your fence or property line

Make this the year you actually *do* put something down on paper. Be brave, or maybe even honest, and enter a summary of triumphs and documentation of the less than stellar performances in the garden. Newbies, this is the time to use the "if I ruled the world" approach—you can always pare down later. In deference to our techno-savvy gardening cohorts, you could actually *use the computer* to keep track of the details of the season.

Sigh, now I've said it. It's too late to retract the idea. As a slightly impaired, or at least challenged, user of electronic devices, this is a huge step for me. Even acknowledging the possibility of entering *gardening details* into one of those cousins of a Black Hole is a major breakthrough. Just ask my children.

Howe're it's done, some kind of record really does come in handy. The savings in dormant bulbs and perennials alone will be worth it. Digging in the off-season to plant or move something else regularly results in bisected bulbs and crown-less perennials. (Let that read as an ear-numbing exclamation of, "We have to replace how many bulbs?") Plus, with measurements in hand, you will have positive proof that four full-sized Colorado Blue Spruces, however diminutive and pretty they look in the little pots, will *not* fit in front of the bay window.

Now take heart, those of you who can't see the current garden for the weeds. Fall is also for wiping the garden clean and putting any disappointment behind you. These months can cancel out the feeling of less-than-happy enthusiasm when you gaze out the window. That daunting vision that once was your garden will soon be gardening history. Ahhh—the chance to start over—the chance to make a running start towards the garden of your dreams.

So *here* is the new gardening year—beginning September 1st-ish. Should your garden be brand digging new or well underway, this is the time to jump right in and make like a gardener. If you wait it will be too late. Okay, not *too* late, but you'll be missing some mighty fine gardening weather!

INITIAL PLANNING

Visualizing and dreaming are the lifeline for gardeners in those daunting planting zones that generally result in frozen ground and piles of snow for months on end. But dreams are the starting point of all gardens—new, or into their fortieth season. It doesn't hurt to do a little drawing as well. It will be a valuable investment of time and effort to make a scale drawing of your entire yard. Use graph paper and place the house roughly in the center of the drawing. Once you have worn through a couple of Pink Pearl erasers and have finally agreed it is pretty darn close to accurate, go over the permanent features with a pen and ruler. Nice straight lines always make it look intentional. And as my dad has always said, "If you can't do it right, make it look intentional."

Permanent features include the house, garage or carport, driveway, sidewalk, post lights, deck or patio (even if you're planning on making a larger one, put in the existing one), non-temporary shed, very large trees that *will* stay no matter what a certain someone else has in mind, and anything else you want to stay in the design. It also helps to make little marks where the hose connections are located—the utility boxes and sprinkler connections as well. And make little double lines to indicate doors and windows to remind you of the view you do or don't want to block with the new trees or fences.

One more helpful purchase when you buy the graph paper is tracing paper. By placing the tracing paper over the ink drawing, you can sketch to your heart's content and if there need to be changes, voilá, no sacrificing yet another Pink Pearl; just slide the paper around or grab a new sheet altogether. If you are, oh say, a detail-oriented individual, this dreaming and planning process will pretty much take up any time left over after all the catalogs have been consumed. All of January, if memory serves me, can be occupied with plan, plan, dream, dream, draw, draw—only occasionally punctuated by a foray out to once again clear the driveway and sidewalk of the new snow.

Lawn

LAWN FROM THE BEGINNING

Everyone wants to make a good first impression and that extends to the front yard of his or her home. For going on 200 years, that good impression has come to mean a beautiful green lawn, in the front and as large as possible. Of course the accepted standard has been that it *must* be the first thing to greet your guests. That look, first created by sheep of the landed gentry in the mother country, was translated to mean, "By jove, we're as good as they are . . . let's show 'em how to grow a *real* lawn!"

That may have been practical once the messy hubbub of becoming our own country subsided; however, not only was that 200 plus years ago, but those folks only lived along the eastern seaboard of this great garden of opportunity. Now, spread out across the continent, we are faced with too much rain or not enough water, terribly cold winters, and scorching dry summers, not to mention frequent hurricanes, tornadoes, and droughts, giving most gardeners in the USA a real challenge to keep up the green appearances of the genteel life of old.

Keeping up appearances with green lawns created a surprising and unintended consequence. It has created a uni-garden look across the land. Denver, Salt Lake City, and Albuquerque struggled mightily to look like Seattle, San Diego, and Des Moines. And green we looked! You could experience the "Big Box Store syndrome" of stepping into any given location and seeing exactly the same suburban landscape found in any other city in America.

More and more homeowners living in the millions of homes built in all parts of the country are now forced to face the undeniable truth—water is a finite resource and we no longer can fill everyone's glass from the few pitchers available. There are other visions of beauty possible beyond the wild green yonder. And the vision might include something that is typical of the geographical location—maybe we could start recognizing Salt Lake City, or any other city, by the plants and details used in the home landscape!

PURPOSE OF LAWNS

So, there are a few considerations to make before deciding to keep the vast expanse of lawn that is already yours. And those are the same considerations which should be taken into account if you are contemplating putting in a vast expanse of new lawn, or a little oasis of green grass for that matter.

TURF GRASS LAWN

The grasses we grow as lawn do *some* things very well:

1. Cool the air.
2. Keep down the dust.
3. Minimize weeds (no, honest!).
4. Keep children clean (versus playing in the mud).

5. Are easily maintained by just about anyone tall enough to guide a lawnmower.

What they don't do well is:

1. Maintain their beauty without consistent additional watering.

2. Maintain a consistent height (without consistent mowing).

3. Manage to thrive where there is constant foot traffic.

4. Adjust to any growing condition that isn't nigh unto perfect for that particular variety of grass.

5. Win *any long term battle* with encroaching weeds unless you are the lawn's constant, doting companion.

Lawns can and do have a glorious role to play in adding to the enjoyment of your own garden world of beauty and contentment. Help them do it well.

GUIDELINES FOR BEAUTIFUL, HAPPY, HEALTHY TURF GRASS LAWNS

1. Only plant grass lawn where it can do at least one of the tasks it does well. Lawn does keep the dirt down and provide great play space, but you would be best served to keep it out from under swings and other play sets. Constant wear puts you right back to battling the mud. This is the perfect space for play chips—those wood chips designed to cushion without giving splinters. And you could put the chips down two or three feet further out from the edge of the play area and reduce the amount of mowing/watering/fertilizing/weeding the lawn area a little bit more.

2. Even if your lawn has lived and invaded a given area of your yard for eighteen years, this could be the time to remove some of it. The location isn't cast in stone you know! (Chuckle!) See if there isn't something that *doesn't* need watering or mowing that would look classy and neat in that area.

3. Try not to make the grass live against concrete, like sidewalks and driveways. Lawn planted out at least two feet from the foundation of the house is easier to trim and stays greener. Even if you don't plant anything in that two foot space along the house, you can put down a weed barrier or mulch, and it will always look neat and tidy. Cutting the lawn back from the edge of the sidewalk not only relieves the stress (on the lawn) and minimizes the weed problem, but it's a great water-conservation step. You no longer have the need (your need, not the lawn's) to water the driveway, sidewalk, and gutter to keep the edges green.

LAWN THAT ISN'T GRASS

Usually we think of and plant turf grass in an area we want to call our lawn. There are other ground cover plants that can take the place of grass in some specific areas. Creeping thyme is a dandy little plant that grows very low to the ground and tolerates some foot traffic. It makes a sort of a 2- to 4-inch tall rolling hill pattern rather than a clipped look with leaves or stems all exactly the same length. Scotch or Irish moss are lovely plants that form a mat so dense over the soil that they look like fine carpet. And they aren't really moss, but fuzzy-looking little flowering plants with teensy white flowers. The thyme has little flowers too, but they vary in shades of pink to lavender depending on the variety. If you only need to actually *cover the ground* but not use the area for play, there are still other plants that fill the bill.

Knowing that turf grass is the recognizable King of the Lawn Plants, we will use it as the plant of choice when talking about lawn. But just keep in mind that maybe there are plants for those selected spots that *don't* need to be mown or weeded as much, but still look green during all the right seasons.

TYPES OF TURF GRASSES

Choose the type of grass you are going to plant based on your climate and the purpose of the lawn. Areas with cool springs, warm or hot summers, and cool autumn temperatures are right for "cool season" grasses like Kentucky bluegrass or fescue. For "cool season" grass, try Bermuda. For areas with warm spring and fall seasons, plus hot summer weather, plant a "warm season" grass like Zoysia.

When buying bluegrass seed, it is advantageous to buy a "blend" or "mixture" instead of only a single variety of bluegrass. "Blend" is a combination of two or more different varieties of just bluegrass. The benefit comes because each variety has a different strength—one greens up earlier in the spring, another is more disease resistant, still another may tolerate hot weather better. "Mixture" indicates different types of grass seed are in the package. For cool season areas that usually means a couple of different varieties of bluegrass, two or three varieties of Fescue, and sometimes a little annual rye grass.

Mixtures can also be helpful in specific areas in your yard. Some are for shady areas and others are specifically mixed for sunny areas.

PREPARATION FOR NEW GRASS LAWNS

Whatever way you choose to install a new lawn—seed, hydro-seed, or sod—the soil preparation should be the same. This is also true when planting in any of the soil types—sandy, clay, or somewhere in between.

- Remove any debris or rocks larger than a ping-pong ball.

- If there are too many weeds to pull, let them grow to about 8 inches tall and mow them down as low as possible, rake up and remove.

- Bring in organic material, either by the bag or truck load. NO plain topsoil. Along the Wasatch Front, getting stuck with "top dirt" instead of "top soil" is almost a given, so stay with the organic material. Lay down *at least* 2 to 3 inches over the entire area to be planted.

- Rototill to a depth of 6 to 7 inches. If a small area is being planted, use a shovel or spading fork.

- Level and water well. If a sprinkling system is being put down, this is the time to trench and lay pipe. Fill the trenches and tamp lightly. Level and water well again.

- Level for the final time and put down sod, hydro-seed, or spread seed.

When you choose sod (pre-grown lawn, cut and sold as rolls or rectangular pieces), water the area well the day before you are going to install the lawn. That, of course, is after you did all the steps of preparation, right? Lay the pieces so the ends don't all line up. The sod should follow the pattern of a brick wall. Water deeply enough to keep the soil beneath the sod moist until the roots begin to grow into the soil below. Water at least daily for about two weeks. When growing on clay soil, it is possible to overwater, so check before you water to make sure the poor sod isn't already sitting in a puddle. After 10–14 days, test one corner of a piece here and there across the lawn to see if the roots are starting to grow into the soil. Lift gently. If you meet with some resistance, roots are growing down into your soil. If the sod comes up like the corner of a throw rug, tamp it back down carefully. Check back in 3 or 4 days. Once the sod begins to grow into your soil, you can reduce watering every other day. And then gradually taper off to a regular watering schedule.

After a couple of weeks, with temperatures start-

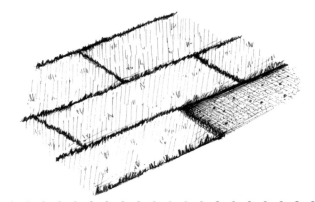

ing to get cooler, it should be possible to cut back to watering every third or fourth day. However, this is no time to put the sod under stress, so watch closely so that it doesn't begin to dry out. After another week of frequent watering, if the roots are attaching well, you can cut back to once every seven to ten days. Utah State University—Utah's agricultural school—makes available the water requirements for a grass lawn during the growing season here along the Wasatch Front. Check your local Extension Office or Master Gardener's Association to see if that information is available for your specific growing area. No additional fertilizer should be applied until after you have been able to mow twice.

PLANTING A NEW LAWN FROM SEED

In a medium to large area, use a rotary or drop spreader so the seed is more evenly distributed rather than tossing it out by hand. Rake lightly over the area, walking backwards to smooth out your footprints. Footprints *now* mean uneven lawn *later*. An empty water-roller (find one at a local rental place) will gently tamp the seeds against the soil. Only the seeds in contact with the soil will grow roots into the soil and survive so there is no reason to put down a deep layer of seeds. Whatever type of seed is used to start the new lawn, water twice daily— even more often during high temperatures or brisk wind. The little grass seeds must stay damp from the time they start to grow until the roots have become established.

To maintain the moisture around the seeds, you can spread mulch *very lightly* over the seed. Be sure to make it a very thin layer of mulch. Grass seed needs water to germinate, as well as good contact with the soil.

Water lightly but often because heavy watering

will float the little seeds in whatever direction the water is flowing. This usually results in a halo of thick grass along the edges of a lawn area but a nearly bald spot in the middle.

Baby new lawn is slow to fill in. Weeds will outgrow the grass at first—don't panic. Pull the largest ones. Wait until after you have mowed the new lawn at least three times if you want to start using a weed killer.

FERTILIZING LAWNS

In most yards fertilizer is dumped on the lawn, whether it's needed or not. Since water dissolves the fertilizer and then moves on through the soil carrying the fertilizer with it, the chemicals percolate down into our water supply. That which doesn't seep into the aquifers runs off and pollutes our rivers and lakes. Plants can only use as much of the nitrogen and other nutrients as they need, and then the rest of the fertilizer often makes its way into lakes causing plants in and near the water to grow excessively. These

> **Bonus Box:** To avoid putting deep footprints into your newly planted lawn, lay a piece of plywood down to do your weeding. That will distribute your weight but do no damage to the little grass plants.

plants can clog waterways and fill smaller ponds. The fertilizers become more concentrated in the water as it moves, because evaporation leaves less water to dilute the salts. These high concentrations of salts can become toxic to plants downstream.

The healthiest and greenest lawn in the spring gets its start when you apply fertilizer in October or November. This is the one time that applying fertilizer to your lawn can make a noticeable difference. Many companies package a "winterizer" type of fertilizer that contain a slow-releasing form of nitrogen. Excellent organic forms of fertilizer are available in large bags for this application. Lawn can put down nice root growth during late fall and even during warm winters. Grass doesn't die during cold temperatures; the growth is just very, very slow. With the additional nitrogen moving so slowly through the soil, the conditions are great for your lawn getting off to an early green start. Be sure any new areas of lawn have been mown three or more times before applying the fall fertilizing.

WATERING LAWNS

Lawns are often grossly overwatered and often carelessly watered to boot. The gallons of water used on lawns are way out of proportion to what is actually needed to keep the grass green and happy. Sprinkling systems that had the clock set for summer watering should be adjusted for the reduced demand because of the cooling temperatures during the fall months. One setting does *not* fit all when using an automatic system. Both seasonal changes and precipitation should govern the timing of the water cycles.

Water bills have gradually taken on "national debt" proportions. My grandfather, while living in Park City, Utah, told my father eighty years ago, "You just watch—someday they'll be charging us for the water we drink and the air we breathe." Halfway there, I guess.

When I was small, Park City water came straight out of the springs and mines. That was the sweetest, coldest water I've ever tasted. And there was no need to treat it—the water was perfectly clear and clean. Now, decades later, the water treatment plant to supply the drinking water to Park City and surrounding areas is huge. And the price of water is still going up.

Remember, lawns are not the monster water wasters—not once has a lawn crept over and turned the sprinkler on and let it run all night. Never has a patch of grass adjusted a sprinkler head so it becomes a car wash for passing motorists. *People* who water improperly are the real water wasters. Consult a local company or extension office to find the most efficient sprinkler or watering system for your area.

CORE AERATION

When things dry out a little in your area, getting someone to core aerate your lawn is an excellent idea. You've probably seen the results of core aerating? It looks like a dog convention used the area for their porta-potty location. If you can possibly stand looking at the cores, it is recommended you leave them in place to naturally breakdown into the soil. Should you, or someone who is alternately covering their eyes and pulling their hair, not be able to wait for the breakdown time to be over, rake the little droppings into your compost pile.

POWER RAKING THE LAWN

There is another power tool occasionally used on lawns—the power rake. Power raking, or de-thatching, can be useful but also has the potential to damage lawns. Thatch, which is *not* just an accumulation of leftover grass clippings, can build up a layer that makes it very difficult for water to penetrate down to soil and root level. Thatch *is* a layer of dead stems and roots that weave together to form something similar to an old thatched roof—hence the name. Thatch accumulates between the soil/root zone and the bottom of the blades of grass. A thin layer (up to one-half inch) of thatch can be beneficial to the lawn because it will help reduce evaporation of water from the soil.

If you are in a warm season grass area, the need to reduce a thatch layer will be greater than in an area that grows primarily bluegrass or fescue for their lawns. To determine if thatch is part of the problem for yellowing and drying spots in your lawn use a sharp blade or trowel to cut down through the grass until you come to the soil layer. A thatch layer will look something like a spongy, tan layer that you can shred apart easily. (In nearly twenty-five years of doing home consultations along the Wasatch Front in Utah, I have only diagnosed one lawn with an accumulation of thatch deep enough to warrant power raking.) The heavy machine has vertical blades that slice through and pull up the layer of thatch.

A good use of power raking is to knock the tops off of the mounds of soil deposited by night crawlers burrowing through compacted or clay soil. When the soil is too dense for the worms to just push their castings into the surrounding soil, they push them to the surface of the soil, creating small mounds. Grass quickly grows in these nutrient rich mounds and creates little ankle-turning hills in the grass. After power raking for either purpose, it will be necessary to overseed the lawn with grass seed to fill the spaces left by the blades of the machine.

WINTERIZING LAWNS

For the last mowing of the season (and good luck guessing when that will be), you can lower the blade on the mower to cut cool season grasses about 1½ inches tall. That is in contrast to the 2 to 3 inches long you were mowing before, right? When temperatures begin to drop down below 80 degrees in the daytime, lawn grass needs less water. Cool season grasses only require 1 to 1½ inches per week in the fall. Natural precipitation will often take care of that for you. However, an exceptionally dry fall will mean you need to keep the hose out or the automatic system on through at least October. That can create the balancing act between keeping the lawn happy and green versus an expensive repair job because an early deep freeze froze your sprinkler pipes. Come down on the side of the sprinklers—lawns are tough, pipes not nearly so tough.

The last chore, repeated many times, is to rake tree residue (leaves and seeds and stems and stuff) off the lawn. This also includes removing old, wet newspapers, the blanket the kids used for the last picnic of the year, dog dishes, three or more trowels, and the occasional baseball cap. Skip any of the items on the list and spring will bring you such a nice surprise—stuff moldering sadly right before your eyes!

The leaves left matting down on the lawn can also lead to snow mold—a pinkish or grey fungus that forms on the lawn when air doesn't circulate around the blades of grass for an entire winter season. Snow that starts accumulating in November and doesn't even try to start melting until March can create the same conditions as matted leaves, both resulting in snow mold. Areas along driveways, sidewalks, and under the eaves of really slippery roofs seem to suffer the most.

> **High on a Mountain Tip:** The weight of heavy snow through the winter may make it necessary to till the garden again in the spring.

The Vegetable Garden

WHERE TO PUT A VEGETABLE GARDEN

If you haven't had a vegetable garden before, fall is an excellent time to get started—yes, fall! Whenever you do get ready to start a vegetable garden, you will need to decide if you would like a traditional single-row garden or a raised-bed garden. If you get the beds made and the soil prepared (or boxes built if you choose to use a raised-bed gardening method), you'll find that you are just that much further ahead in the spring when it is time to plant.

As you survey your gardening kingdom, make note of where the sun shines directly on the soil for the most hours during the day. That is the best place for a vegetable/herb garden. The area should also be away from trees because not only do they cast shade for some part of the day, but the tree roots will out-compete the smaller plants for water and nutrients. Sometimes that most sunny place is right smack dab in the middle of the lawn.

SINGLE-ROW GARDENS

If you choose to have a single-row vegetable garden, now is a good time to prepare the soil. Clear it of any grass or weeds, and rototill or hand dig. At the same time add organic matter until the soil is a good, workable texture. Then, come spring, you can start gardening just as soon as the soil dries and you can use a rake to smooth out the bumps.

INTENSIVE GARDENING

Intensive planting—where seeds are scattered in a block rather than in rows—has some advantages. Every part of the soil is busy growing plants, with none of the soil reserved to channel water or walk on. The closely planted veggies shade the soil, limiting weed growth and slowing water evaporation. These beds are often raised growing beds, adding the advantage of soil warming earlier in the spring and better water drainage through the soil.

RAISED-BED GARDENS

Many people are choosing to garden using a raised-bed method. Gardening in raised beds simply means that you grow your plants above the level of the ground. This is usually achieved by building a structure—such as a wooden frame and filling it with soil. You can also use bricks, concrete blocks, and many other materials to build your raised beds. You're really only limited by your imagination and the space you have in your yard. It's also possible to purchase raised beds commercially or simply construct your own. For a more informal garden, raised beds can also be created by simply piling up the soil to form the beds.

ADVANTAGES OF A RAISED BED

There are many advantages to a raised bed over the traditional single-row garden:

- A true raised-bed garden never needs tilling because the soil does not become compacted—you don't walk on a raised bed. Soil compaction can reduce crop yields up to 50 percent. Water, air, and roots all have difficulty moving through soil compressed by tractors, tillers, or the gardener's boots.

- Planting can take place earlier in the spring since there is no need to wait for perfect weather or for the soil to dry out. A raised-bed garden simply thaws and dries out quicker.

- A raised-bed garden takes up less space, yet the same amount of produce can be grown in that reduced area.

- A raised bed can be an attractive focal point in a landscape and can be as simple or elaborate as desired.

- A raised-bed garden has fewer weeds and therefore takes less time out of a busy schedule.

CHARACTERISTICS OF RAISED BEDS

Whether you choose to corral your raised beds with a structure, or simply mound your soil, you should follow the same simple guidelines.

- A bed should be no wider than 4 feet to be easily reached from both sides, but the length can be as desired.

- If the bed is up against a fence or a wall where you can only reach from one side, keep the bed two feet wide.

- Aisles between beds may be left in sod, mulched, or even paved with stone, gravel, or brick.

- Dig out any grass or weeds in the area where the bed itself will be located.

- Raised beds require excellent organic soil. If using existing soil, mix in at least 3–4 inches of good organic matter. Or, if you want, use the organic mix solely in place of the existing soil.

- Carefully consider the orientation of the beds. Tall crops should be planted on the north side of a bed to prevent shading any low-growing, sun-loving plants. A north-south orientation is best for low-growing crops, allowing direct sunlight to both sides of the bed. Beds that will contain taller crops such as corn, pole beans, or trellised tomatoes might do better in an east-west layout. Lower-growing crops could be planted on the south side of the bed and still get full sun. Conversely, shade-loving plants such as lettuce should be planted where they will be shaded by taller crops.

UNSTRUCTURED RAISED BEDS

To create a raised bed, mix in organic matter at the same time the garden is first tilled. Dig walkways down with the soil thrown up creating the planting area. The beds should be four feet wide at the base, tapered slightly to top. Why? So the soil won't slide into the path. You can cover the entire bed with organic mulch like dry grass clippings to further prevent soil erosion. The mulch will also reduce compaction from rain and sprinkler irrigation. All care of the bed is done from the paths. You can keep your feet on the path and still work all areas of the garden. When you need to add more organic matter, you can dig it in by hand. However, if you have a small tiller you love to use, you could use it in this type of bed. Just reshape the beds and smooth out the soil when you finish tilling.

> **Bonus Box:** The soil used to fill deeper raised beds should not be mixed with any of your garden soil because garden soil can possibly contain disease organisms and will certainly compact too heavily. The soil in these boxes needs to be made from a combination of several different good organic amendments, such as a variety of compost and peat moss with vermiculite added to hold moisture and keep the soil texture light.

STRUCTURED RAISED BEDS

To contain a raised bed, it is better to use only untreated lumber. And, for heaven's sake, don't use railroad ties that are covered in creosote, but you *can* use cinderblock, man-made lumber, bricks, rocks, or vinyl. After digging out grass, you may choose to put down a weed barrier, then build the raised bed on top. Next, fill the raised bed with good organic soil. That weed barrier can be as simple as laying down a large piece of cardboard. The cardboard will eventually disintegrate, but will first choke out any weeds that try to grow. Make sure the barrier extends beyond the edge of the box and growing soil for at least six inches. Otherwise, the grass will sneak right into the box and try to reclaim its territory. I think the best weed barrier really is cardboard, but before you put it down, mix in the good organic matter with your existing soil. That way, when the cardboard disintegrates, the plant roots can keep right on growing.

Raised-bed boxes can be any height you want them to be from only 8 inches to 3 feet or more. They can also be the height of two cinder blocks stacked one on top of the other, creating a garden where you can sit on the edge saving your knees. Some of us can still kneel in the garden, but that's not the problem—the problem is getting back up! And if your back dictates that your bending days are over, another great advantage of raised beds is that they can also be constructed high enough so you can enjoy gardening while standing up. It can also be made the right height so that it is wheelchair accessible. In extra tall gardens, fill the bottom with whatever you want that allows good drainage such as rocks, gravel, or road base—even packing peanuts can be used in a small garden! On top of this filler, add a weed barrier and a few inches of sand topped with 8–10 inches of good organic growing soil.

WATERING A RAISED-BED GARDEN

Confining your watering to just the raised beds and

not the paths (simplifying watering and conserving water in the process) also reduces disease by keeping the water on the soil instead of leaf surfaces. There are several methods of watering to choose from—soaker hoses, drip irrigation, or even by hand using a nozzle on a hose. If push comes to shove, you can use an overhead sprinkler, but it will negate some of the advantages of your raised bed garden. Keep the soil moist and don't allow it to dry out. Check below the surface to see how much water is needed. This will vary according to the age of the plants, temperature, and the weather.

SQUARE FOOT GARDENING

A modified raised-bed method, called Square Foot Gardening, adds even more advantages over the usual row and furrow way of vegetable gardening.

> **High on a Mountain Tip:** Match the requirements of plants to the various micro-climates of your yard. For instance, the south side of your house gets full sun all day long, while the north side is shady most of the day. The west side gets sun in the middle of the day and stays hot until the sun sets while the east side is sunny in the morning and shady in the afternoon.

This method, invented by Mel Bartholomew, is a simple yet versatile system of raised-bed gardening that is characterized by a square foot grid on the top of each garden box to aid in plant spacing. The same amount of vegetables can be grown in only 20 percent of the space of a traditional row garden. This method saves on time, water, seeds, and work, and is very productive. (See squarefootgardening.com.)

> **Bonus Box:** Create your own small microclimate to accommodate plants usually too tender for your area. This can be done by building a small wall, a windbreak with trees or shrubs, or creating a new planting bed on the south side of the house, patio, or sidewalk. Mound up low-lying areas where cold air settles.

Fruit

FRUIT—A BOTANICAL LESSON

The word "fruit" usually conjures up a mental picture of bananas, apples, and cherries. It also should provoke visions of pumpkins, cucumbers, and tomatoes!

Technically, a strawberry is a swollen stem, and it is the fruit that gets stuck between your teeth! Same with apples—we eat the stem and throw away the "fruit" which is the core. (See Mini Glossary: fruit, page 13).

Whether we are speaking of peaches or eggplants, they are both fruit. Often, "fruit" is thought of as sweet, not savory. Fruit *can* be a dessert and a treat, and we often expect only vegetables to be savory and not eaten with the sweet part of the meal. The mind-set is to segregate some fruit as vegetables and some as "real fruit," as most people accept the distinction. It saves a lot of confusion if you wait to clarify the distinction between fruit and vegetable as a tidbit of botanical knowledge that can be shared in a group gathering when the conversation starts to lag! In this book we'll mostly use the recognized separation between the two. Of course, then there is the pumpkin . . . fruit or vegetable? Soup or pie?

RAKE UP FALLEN FRUIT

You should pick up the leaves and old fruit that have fallen under or near vines, bushes, and trees. Put them into areas for composting unless you have had insect or disease problems. Any apples or pears with little holes in them should go straight to the garbage. The little brown holes usually indicate a worm is living

> **High on a Mountain Tip:** Cold will settle in low-lying areas freezing crops while surrounding areas will not freeze.

there. If you let the fallen fruit remain under the trees, you'll be contributing several snug little winter chalets for the bugs and diseases that would love to share your property for the winter. They will emerge happy and ready to attack your plants come spring.

RASPBERRIES

Raspberries grow best in a cool summer environment—like around Bear Lake in Utah! But they can still produce nicely in warmer areas. To moderate that hot summer afternoon sun, put the plants on the east side of a wall or fence that is on the west side of your yard. That gives them full morning and early afternoon sun but a little shade in the hottest part of the day. It might be possible to find raspberry plants that are in pots this time of year. But if you wait until spring, nurseries will have the same varieties in bare root stock. This way they are less expensive and they root easily. In the fall you can prepare the bed and decide what kind, if any, supports you will put up along the raspberry bed.

All raspberries multiply by sending out underground runners that pop up as new canes—everywhere. It is very difficult to keep the plants in tidy little rows. There are several methods for keeping them controlled and you may come up with yet another one in coming years as you wrestle the raspberry canes for the best two out of three.

CORRALLING RASPBERRIES

Raspberries can be supported by running wires between two or three or more posts depending on how long or wide your berry patch is. Make the wires approximately 18 inches apart and you can weave the canes between them. Place the berry plants between the two sets of poles and wires and let them grow more loosely. Keep the space between the "berry fences" 2–3 feet wide so you can reach the middle fairly easily.

You can also gather the canes from each plant together into little teepees so they will stand up without any other support. Or you can just let them

ramble where they have a mind to if you have plenty o' room to spare. Just remember, most varieties have nasty little prickles that aren't easy to push hand and arms through.

PRUNING RASPBERRIES

If you were able to plant raspberries in the spring, it is likely you have yet to see a raspberry to eat. But the upside of that is the new raspberry canes won't need pruning now or next spring.

The varieties we call "ever-bearing" usually produce a good crop of berries around June and then a few more later in the summer and more into fall. Try Heritage or September varieties if you're interested in a few berries for shortcake or some on your cereal or bowl of ice cream.

June-bearing raspberries go all out for the early crop and are then done for the year. If you would like enough to make raspberry jam or syrup, try the variety called Canby—sometimes called the Bear Lake Raspberry. The canes produce heavily and have very few prickles on the stems.

Raspberry canes need careful specific pruning or you might end up with all "rasp" (canes) and no "berries." Canes only bear once, so you can cut those that have had fruit on them right to the ground. Remove any tiny canes smaller around than a pencil ,even if they didn't bear fruit, because it strengthens the remaining canes. Do this pruning once you have picked all of the berries that the cane will bear for the year.

June Bearing: Each cane must be considered and removed once it is done bearing for the year, along with the tiny, weak canes. Late fall or very early spring is the preferred time to prune this type of raspberry.

Ever-bearing: You can choose between two techniques for pruning this type of raspberry.

1. Like the June bearers, you can take off the individual canes as they finish producing. Those canes that bear in the early summer will be different in appearance from the ones that have borne fruit in the fall. Check to see if there are tiny green flower buds on the ends of canes or side canes—they look a little like tiny pointy hats. Leave those canes to produce later. Remove the woodier-looking stems with the dried cores left from when you picked the earlier berries.

2. The second method can be used on ever-bearing raspberries either in mid to late October, or very early in March. Cut the entire patch completely to the ground. Yes, every cane! The canes that come back later in the spring (honest, they do grow back) will bear fruit only in the late summer. Okay, this sort of turns them into the equivalent of June bearers, but all the raspberries ripen in the fall rather than June. The real advantage of this method over removing individual canes one at a time, is that you can completely clean out the raspberry patch and tend to the weed removal, dividing some of the plants and digging others

out to reclaim the path that once let you into the middle of the patch—stuff like that.

PRUNING FRUIT TREES

During the growing season, some branches may have died on the fruit trees. Dead branches can be pruned off anytime you notice them. But remember—leave no stubs or stumps. The major pruning and shaping of the fruit trees should be done in the early spring. Other than those dead branches and

> **Warning:** DON'T use the clear-cut method with June bearing raspberries or you'll never see another berry again.

the one that poked you in the eye for the last time, pruning should wait until late winter or early spring for the fruit trees.

WINTERIZING FRUIT TREES— PROTECTION

Fruit trees need little care in the fall months. Perhaps in September, the peach tree branches will need support from underneath because someone forgot to thin the peaches last June. But other than that, it's mostly a matter of cleaning up all of the fallen fruit.

All trees will benefit from a late-season deep watering. This should be done after all peaches/nectarines/apples have been harvested. If you have a peach or nectarine tree, stop watering for a couple of weeks before harvesting to help the peaches/nectarines (nectarines are just naked peaches with no fuzz) develop stronger flavor. Later in the fall, let a hose or sprinkler run very slowly out around the drip line so the water will penetrate deeply. This may take several hours for a large tree. If possible, the watering line should be all the way around the tree. When half the tree branches hang over the fence, just be concerned with your half. Don't put the water right up to the trunk. There are no roots there that need the water and the moisture might cause disease problems in the trunk or roots of the tree.

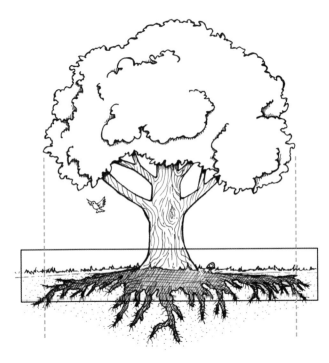

In areas with very cold winter temperatures, zero degrees and below, painting or wrapping the trunks of young fruit trees will help minimize Southwest Winter Damage, sometimes just called winter scald or damage. (See page 41 for technique.)

WINTERIZING GRAPES

Grapes are self-sufficient for the next four or five months. They don't need tending at all—other than raking up their leaves and into the compost or green bin. And then there are those crafty type people who might like to raid the backyard vineyard for the dormant vines. I understand crafters can make any number of . . . well, *thingeys* out of the grapevines. (I acknowledge that I am craft-impaired and really don't want to do a thing about it. My crafting friends, rolling their eyes and wagging their heads, forgive me for my lack of intent to become "one" with the glitter. They content themselves with a sneaky addition of a rhinestone or two on my gardening apron from time to time.)

Anyway, the grapes will need a good cutting back next spring anyway, so go ahead and fold, bend, spindle, and mutilate the vines all you want. Ahem, I mean, you crafty folks are sure to fashion them into decorative delights. Probably with glitter and rhinestones, I'm betting.

Harvest Time

VEGETABLES—PICK THEM AT THEIR TASTIEST

The garden that *grew* during the earlier part of the season could actually mean you will be enjoying harvest time during these autumn days. Harvest also assumes that there was, in fact, a planting and a watering and a weeding part of the process prior to this harvest step in the gardening adventure.

If you took a stab at a vegetable garden *and* you had some success with your plants and seeds, this is the time of year you've been waiting for. Peak production of many vegetables has been reached—that is, if you really did plant and talk to your garden plants (talking is optional, but helpful). Maybe not so much *peak* production, but hey, two tomatoes, never-ending zucchini, and one little jalapeño pepper still count as a harvest. Don't be discouraged!

Every garden has to start somewhere.

Temperatures and day length dictate the end of the growing season for the tender veggies and fruit. As with the rest of the tender veggie garden, melons and summer squash can be protected from the first couple of light frosts that come this time of year, but that doesn't change the fact that there just aren't enough hours of sunlight during the day to do much more ripening after the average date of first frost in your area has come and gone. (See Frost Chart on page 141.)

How can you tell when those fruits and vegetables are at their prime and ready to harvest? There is often a window that may only last a few days and you certainly want to eat or preserve those veggies when they are at their best. Here's a description of some of the most common vegetables and fruits typically grown in home gardens:

Beans

Green beans—the color green that is—are not supposed to look like a beaded necklace in a little green sleeve. The pods should be picked when they are still straight, without bulges. Same goes for yellow or purple "green" beans.

> **High on a Mountain Tip:** Living at high altitudes (5000 feet and above) can easily cut short the growing season even before the first part of September. And for you folks that delight in your longer growing season, just because the *average* first frost date is the middle of October, it doesn't mean the early part of that average isn't going to sneak up and flatten your garden about the first of September. So be prepared to cover your garden and protet from the first frost. Often, there will be several frost-free weeks iafterward in which to continue enjoying the harvest.

Beets, Turnips, Rutabagas

Beets should be between the size of a golf ball and a tennis ball when you pull them. And the same goes for turnips and rutabagas. (Don't knock them until you've tried them. They really are good in a stew, Cornish Pasty, or medley of roasted root vegetables. Notice they are vegetables? You are eating the roots! Carrots and onions are veggies, too. Technically you are eating an onion *bulb*, but it still counts as a vegetable.)

Carrots

Carrots can stay in the ground even after the first frost—making storage from summer to about November a snap. Of course you can harvest as soon as they are big enough to look like carrots. But, how do you tell, since they are underground? Pull one and check! Just go out and get one when it's time for the Sunday roast or a picnic veggie plate. If your soil has dried out a little, use a spading fork to loosen the soil before trying to pull up the carrots. This will prevent you from coming away with just a handful of the lacy leafy greens.

Cucumbers

Cucumbers—another of the lovely fruits—play a hide-and-seek game with you, and the winner gets the cucumber. Vines that were chugging out four, five, or six cucumbers a day can suddenly stop altogether. No new blossoms, no fruit, nothing to pick at all. That signals the start of the game. You need to very carefully, perhaps even on bended knee, search under *every* leaf and stem until you find the bulging, no longer little, cucumber that is probably even turning a little yellow on one side. Pick that blasted over-blown cucumber and it will be like releasing water behind a plugged watering furrow—*whoosh*—

CORNISH PASTY

My grandfather worked in mines in England and came to work the mines in Park City, Utah where he taught my grandmother to make these rugged full meal turnovers. She wrapped them in paper and then Grandpa heated the pasties over a carbide lamp down in the depths of the mines. He was originally from Devonshire, but that is a stone's throw from Cornwall where these little pies originated.

For our pasties in my mom's kitchen, we added onions, and shame be known, used ground beef. That is totally against all that is pasty—meat is to be cut into small chunks to be proper. And I have added another slight to the "true" pasty—I grate my potatoes.

Oh my. That just isn't right, I hear my forebears muttering—proper vegetables for a pasty are always sliced.

And a proper pasty needs a tough crust, not a dainty flaky one. Miners would kid that they could tell a proper pasty because it would hold together even if it fell to the bottom of the shaft!

MOM'S VERSION OF A CORNISH PASTY

½ Cup sliced or diced onion
1 small turnip, grated or diced
2 medium potatoes, grated or diced
1 carrot, grated
1 pound of ground beef
salt and pepper to taste

1. Using your favorite recipe for pie crust, prepare enough for a two-crust pie. (Don't be gentle, remember, it should be heavy/tough dough.) Roll dough and cut into 8-inch diameter circles. This should make 2–4 pasties. You can also make larger circles for fewer pasties.

2. Place a layer of onions and carrots down the middle of each circle of dough. Salt and pepper lightly. Next add a layer of potatoes. Salt and pepper lightly. Then add little pieces of the ground beef. Salt lightly. Top with turnips.

3. Bring the two edges of the crust together so they meet in the middle like the laces of a football. Crimp the two edges together tightly; secure so the ends don't leak. Make a small slit on one side of the seam. Place on a lightly-buttered baking sheet.

4. Bake at 415 degrees for 20 minutes then reduce temperature to 325 degrees and bake for another 25 to 35 minutes until golden brown.

5. Miners enjoyed their pasty by wrapping it paper and reheating it by their carbide lamp 6 hours later at lunch time, but you can eat yours straight from the oven!

overnight blossoms appear, and in less that a week you are back to making little cucumber sandwiches! Pickling cucumbers usually have little pokey spines on them and can be picked from the time they are two inches long. Slicing cucumbers, usually the ones with the smooth skin, can be picked when they are from 6–16 inches long, depending on the variety.

Melons

Remember, melons, don't store at all well! Therefore, eating is the only answer to the question of what to do with them once they are ripe. But that brings us to yet another question—how do you tell when they *are* ripe?

Watermelons should be good to eat when the little pigtail tendril opposite the stem that hooks the watermelon to the vine is dried up *and* the underside of the melon has changed from a dull cream color to yellow.

Rather than, or sometimes in addition to the tendril checking, some gardeners prefer the "thump-thump" method. An unripe melon is supposed to sound like you just thumped somebody's head. I've heard it said "your own" head, but I think that complicates the method by the echo you hear through your skull. (At least that's my excuse for not getting the underripe diagnosis "correct.") Ripeness is signaled when the thump sounds like a solid whack against your chest. The oh-rats-it's-too-ripe sound is like you thwacked your abdomen.

I am a horrible thumper/whacker. Or rather, I'm a horrible thump/whack listener. No way can I get any sound from a watermelon that even remotely resembles a thwack on the human body. Not that it concerns me. Watermelon and I don't get along anyway, so I don't worry about judging the melon to be ripe or not. I eat cantaloupe instead.

Some melons "slip" or come off of the vine easily when ready. Many muskmelons and cantaloupes do this. It is an easy way to judge the melons—just lift and tilt, and if they drop off the stem easily, they are ready! Sometimes it does lead to over-ripe fruit because *nobody* went out and checked *yesterday or the day before* when they were perfect, but now they are mushy and have a yucky taste.

Corn

Most corn has been harvested by September, but if you have late corn that is still ready to pick, check page 114 for a description on how to tell if it is ripe.

Onions

Onions can be pulled as soon as they are pencil-sized to use as green onions, called scallions. Leave them in the ground with enough space, and some of, them will grow to "slice them for a hamburger" size. They should be pulled before a hard frost.

Peppers

Ripe peppers have a much sweeter taste than the not-quite-ripe green ones. Sweet or bell peppers will change color when they are ripe! So be daring and let them become red, yellow, orange, or purple peppers. Hot peppers change color too. The color changes when they approach their full size.

The hottest parts of the pepper are the seeds and the whitish ribs on the inside of the fruit. (There's that fruit thing again! Seeds inside = fruit.) You can tone down the heat a little by removing those parts before chopping or slicing or stuffing or whatever tasty thing you do with your peppers. And do be careful when handling those fiery gems. Be sure to wear gloves and remember to wash your hands very well with soap and water before rubbing your eyes, or nose, or any other *sensitive* part of your anatomy!

Tomatoes

One of the reasons gardeners and eaters love home-grown tomatoes is that there is actually flavor in them thar red/yellow/orange "tomaters." That wonderful taste difference can be explained at least in part because home gardeners actually let the tomatoes ripen before picking them. Commercially produced tomatoes must be picked green so they can survive the long journey to your local market, hence the flavorless crunch of store-bought offerings.

But to really rank higher on the delight scale than than those from the grocery produce department, tomatoes must be picked when just perfectly ripe—or very close so they can ripen on your counter.

Tomatoes need to be uniformly the color intended (red, yellow, orange, purple, and so on), and need to nearly fall into your palm when you put your hand under the fruit and lift with a slight twist. Sometimes the little stem comes with the tomato—sometimes not—it doesn't matter. But if you're tugging rather vigorously before the tomato reluctantly gives up its "home, home on the vine," you should consider coming back in a day or two and try it again. Remember, actual taste is worth waiting for.

Summer Squash

Summer squash, such as zucchini and yellow crookneck, were never intended to be baseball bat stand-ins. Nor were they meant to be garage door propper-uppers no matter how convenient they seem to be. No, they are meant to one of the culinary delights coming from your garden. In order for them to be at their tender best, pick zucchini when they are a maximum of six to eight inches long. The baby squash that are so expensive in the store are yours for the picking, too. Just snap off any summer squash when they are only 2 to 3 inches long and you'll have a gourmet's delight.

If your family is from Italy (or not) and has a traditional recipe for stuffed zucchini you may want to let one, two, or more approach 12 inches long. This will take only an extra day or two, so don't let your family heritage lull you into a lackadaisical approach to squash harvest. Vigilance is the watchword for tending the summer squash plot. And when picking, always keep an eye out for the one hiding under one of the huge leaves—oh, it's there all right. And if left alone to continue its zucchini or yellow squash tendency, it will not only turn into that baseball bat, but because the seeds inside are starting to mature, the entire plant will concentrate on that one fruit, and stop producing the little squash that are *soooo* good to eat.

HARVEST FROM FRUIT TREES

Apples

Cut an apple in half to check for ripeness—dark brown seeds indicate a ripe apple, but maybe still not at the peak of sweetness. Many apples are sweetest after the first couple of light frosts.

Peaches

For peaches to be at their sweetest the sunshine should hit the fruit. Proper pruning in the early spring should create an open-centered tree to expose the fruit to the sun. A ripe peach should fall into your hand when you put your palm under the fruit and lift up and twist slightly. The fruit should give slightly when you squeeze gently. They develop their sweetest flavor when ripened on the tree, so don't be in a hurry to pick them.

Pears

Pears need to be picked while still green, both in color and ripeness. If left to ripen on the tree, pears develop "stone cells" which feel very gritty when you chew the fruit. Pick the pears just as the little tiny spots or dots appear on the skin. Put them on the counter or in a paper bag to finish ripening. Check every day and when they are yellow and give slightly when you squeeze them, they are ready to eat.

Plums

A gentle squeeze and then a taste test will let you know if they are ripe—and will really jolt the old taste buds if they aren't!

WINTER VEGETABLE STORAGE

Carrots

Carrots can be left in the ground long after the season has slipped from fall to winter—in fact, all the way through the winter if you have a way to keep the ground around them from freezing solid. Bales of hay over the rows work great for this purpose! It *is* getting harder to find the local hay bale distributor in many locations, so try some black bags filled with leaves. If your one and only young maple tree merely dropped a total of twenty-two leaves, I'm sure some neighbor will happily part with a few of their bags. Then, when you need a couple of sweet crunchy carrots for the veggie tray you're taking to the neighborhood party just go out and brush the snow off the black bags. Lift the bag and dig or pull the carrots!

Winter Squash

Winter squash, including pumpkin, Hubbard, acorn, butternut, banana, and the many other varieties, are able to stay on the vine long after they may actually be ripe enough to enjoy. When the rind, or outer skin, gets tough it makes them perfect for storage over the—are you ready for this—winter! Thus, we call them *winter* squash. Winter storage doesn't mean leaving them outside though. The long winter cold will turn them into a pile of rather disgusting mush by spring.

Check for storage readiness by gently pushing your

fingernail into the rind (outer skin layer). You could also use a butter knife if fingernails aren't your long suit. If the resulting scratch quickly fills with liquid, the pumpkin or other squash won't last long in storage after being picked and it likely isn't quite ripe. Check again in a week or so. Once the scratch doesn't immediately weep liquid, you can cut the squash from the vine. You can still leave it on the vine in the garden until frost is near if storage space is at a premium. To keep it at it's best as long as possible after cutting, be sure to leave at least two inches of the stem attached to the top of the vine. This eliminates one source of decay by allowing the stem to stay tight on the end of the squash instead of creating a circular wound. And it makes a great handle for a Jack O' Lantern's lid.

A very light frost won't hurt the squash left in the field even if it really does a number on the leaves and green vines. "When the frost is on the pumpkin" often is said to mean the ending of the growing season and beginning of putting the produce into storage or on the table for dinner. A light frost hits when the temperatures fall around 30 to 32 degrees. A freeze on the other hand signals temperatures plummeting below 25 or 26 degrees.

Do pick them before a hard freeze turns them to soggy pulp, however. Wash the squash with soapy water containing 1 part chlorine bleach to 10 parts water to remove the soil and kill the pathogens on the surface to increase the length of storage time. Make sure the squash is well dried before curing. Put your winter squash in a warm (75–85 degrees or so), dry place to cure for a couple of weeks. After that, any place that stays dry and about 50–55 degrees will keep them for weeks or even months. The back bedroom with the closed off heating vent used only when Grandma comes to visit is perfect. The coolest part of the room is the floor so under the bed makes for great squash storage.

Always store squash away from apples, since apples produce ethylene gas as they ripen, which speeds up the ripening process in pumpkins, thus decreasing their shelf life. Check the fruits regularly and remove the ones that are rotten or going soft. Just as one rotten apple will spoil the barrel, one rotten squash will spread the rot to all the others. Don't place them on a moist concrete floor; use boards or some other means to keep them off the floor. Don't stack the squash one on top of another—you need to allow for air circulation between them.

Post-Harvest Clean Up

Extra Bonus Box: Ethylene Gas—a naturally occurring gas that speeds up ripening of vegetation is released from apples. When apples are stored near potatoes it will cause the potatoes to begin to sprout, but will speed up ripening pears or avocados.

VEGETABLE GARDEN

Once you have given in to the inevitable conclusion that your garden is done for the season, clean-up efforts should begin. You don't have to wait until your produce has been reduced to brown stems, slimy old fruit, and black-as-an-eight-ball zucchini before starting to close down the garden. You can decide the garden is done any old time you want.

A friend of mine loves zucchini bread, zucchini cookies, and zucchini cakes. The idea of actually eating a zucchini squash in a salad, sautéed, baked, or any other form where you could actually tell it *was zucchini*, seems absurd to her. Kay calculates that she uses roughly 24 cups of grated zucchini in her baking recipes per year.

When her two zucchini plants come into production, she lets the squash get about 12 to 14 inches long and then picks them. Her food processor stands at the ready. Zip, and the squash are grated coarsely. Another zip and the plastic bags are closed, each one containing 2 cups of grated zucchini. After a few zip sessions, her quota is filled for the year and sits comfortably tucked into her freezer.

Then she is off to the garden and pulls out the zucchini plants!

"Whoa!" you say. Those are perfectly fine plants that still have a lot of little zucchini left to give. Maybe so, but they are now filling a lot of space in her garden that could move on to something else— like beans, for instance. So, it's off with their heads and into the compost for the zucchini plants. The next day she *does* plant her late beans, and she never feels the guilt of sharing (let that read *dumping*) a pile of summer squash on a table at work. Nor do her neighbors dread the season of Zucchini Ditching in the vicinity of *her* garden. At least they know the squash didn't come from Kay!

There are valid reasons for pushing yourself (or willing or coercing others) to clean all of the plant debris from your garden at the end of harvest time. Insects and diseases just love all of that decaying mess of stems, leaves, and missed produce with a few late season weeds thrown in to boot. It makes for a perfect over-wintering condo—with a moist, dark, warm, fully-stocked pantry. Even if the grown-up insects have left or died, their offspring in the larvae or egg stages will appreciate the accommodations.

As early as Labor Day in September, some gardeners start the garden cleanup. That may seem a titch early, but these people don't get caught pulling frozen marigolds out of four inches of snow! And dry pumpkin vines are infinitely easier to drag to the compost pile than the soggy, slimy vines left after two or three hard frosts.

Some of the old vegetation and produce can be tilled into the garden along with the season's addition of organic matter. A warning though—any plants that showed signs of disease should be excluded as well as any weeds that are still holding onto their seeds. It's to the green landfill for stuff in those categories. It's best to exclude them from *your* compost pile as well. Very few homemade compost piles get hot enough to kill the disease organisms and weed seeds.

So when *is* the best time to do fall cleanup in the veggie garden? Whenever you, time, and enough energy all come together!

Ornamental Trees and Shrubs

FALL PRUNING

Trees, shrubs, and woody herbs make up the visual structure of the garden. Their strength of character *and* their flaws start to show up this time of year. Leaves can mask a multitude of problems in the garden. Broken limbs and branches suddenly pop out from what once looked like a uniformly shaped beautiful globe of green. Pruning of dead branches is an anytime chore—just use proper pruning techniques and don't leave any stubs or stumps. This is done by cutting the dead branch back to the next larger or smaller living branch. To check if the branch is alive, scratch the bark with your fingernail—you should see green just under the surface.

PLANTING

This is a great season to plant shrubs and trees. In Utah, there is a terrific organization that sponsors Plant a Family Tree Month every year. Participating nurseries donate a percentage of the sale of every tree to buy more trees for projects like parks and urban forest plantings. There are usually great sale prices on many trees to add to the incentive for planting. Check in your local area to see if a similar program exists.

From the tree's point of view, fall is a wonderful time of year to go in the ground. The soil is warm, precipitation is more likely, and the air is cool. In fact, long after the air is registering freezing temperatures, the soil is still open (not frozen) and perfect for good root growth. Then, to make fall growing even better, all those pesky leaves fall from the deciduous trees ,leaving most of the energy for the growing roots. Of course, this does lead to the final gardening act of the year—raking up those pesky leaves!

HOW TO PLANT A TREE

> **High on a Mountain Tip:**
> Keep out the cold from your home by planting a windbreak on whichever side of your home the prevailing winter winds blow. Plant evergreens because they keep their needles year-round.

In the springtime, bare root trees are available for planting, but not in the fall. (See page 92). The trees available in the fall are containerized—meaning they have been put in a container and allowed to grow forming a root ball.

As you get ready to plant your tree, remember that the most important half hour in a tree's life is when it comes out of the pot and the planting process is finished. And of that thirty minutes, twenty-five ought to be spent digging a proper hole.

The hole should only be as deep as the soil in the container. That way the tree roots will set on undisturbed soil. If you get carried away thinking if a 12-inch hole is good, then a 36-inch-deep hole ought to be better, there will be a lot of back filling to do before the tree sits where it belongs near ground level. Seems like all that good, soft soil ought to be good for the tree, but the problem is that it settles as you water over the coming weeks, and the crown of the tree ends up way too deep. Moisture in the soil sitting around the crown encourages disease organisms and the tree is likely to develop Crown or Root Rot. These can often kill the tree in a short time.

Digging the hole with the proper width will give you the workout that you escaped when digging the shallow hole. The width of your hole should be at least twice the width of the container and three times would be even better. By digging out that much soil or dirt you give the roots a fighting chance to get well established. The process of filling the hole is almost as critical to tree health as was digging it properly.

Before you put the tree into the hole, drag out the hose and fill the hole with water. This will serve two purposes. First, the soil surrounding and at the bottom of the hole won't be absorbing the water you put in the hole for the tree roots. Second, you get a chance to see what kind of drainage the soil has.

If the water is still in the hole eight hours later, you need to reconsider how and where you plant the tree:

1. You can try a different spot in the yard, but fill the hole with water there, too.

2. You can break up the soil of the bottom of the hole with a spading fork or pry bar. Just DON'T just dig the hole deeper.

3. You can shove the soil back in the hole. Now bring in a load of organic material and create a raised bed that is 8 inches higher than the surrounding area. Mix the organic addition with the existing soil, don't just spread it on top. Make the raised bed at least 4–6 feet wide and at least that long. Now dig that hole again!

If the water drains from this hole in less than eight hours, you are ready to plant your tree.

It's tempting to back fill the hole with really, good rich compost, but it's doubtful, though, if that good rich stuff comes anywhere near to matching the soil you just took out of the ground. With the hole filled with great soil, why would the roots want to grow out into the wild frontier of your regular garden soil? Actually, they don't and they won't! Roots are very slow to grow from one soil texture to another. So you've actually created a large flower pot that will contain the roots for years to come. If you do want to add some compost to the soil from the hole, do it in a ratio of about 1 shovelful of compost to 5–6 shovelfuls of existing soil. Mix the organic matter with the soil before you start filling the hole.

Fill the hole halfway with soil and settle the soil with water to remove large pockets of air. Roots can't live in the large air spaces and can die when they try to grow through them.

Fill the hole to the top and water again. The way you fill and place the soil at the top of the hole is critical to tree survival.

It is reasonable to mound the soil around the planting hole, creating a moat to hold the water.

The trouble with the moat is that sometimes you fill the soil so it slopes down towards the tree trunk. No matter how carefully you water, the slope causes the water to puddle around the trunk. This creates soggy bark and allows disease to set in.

The bank of soil is a good idea as long as the soil slopes away from the trunk and then back up to the rim. Kind of like a doughnut with the tree in the hole in the middle.

There is no doubt that planting large trees with trunks 2–3 inches or more across, adds to the landscape sooner than a young, smaller tree. There is a trade-off, however. Figure on about one year per inch of trunk diameter before top growth (leaves and branches) begins. Large trees pretty much look the same for three to four years while their smaller counterparts will have begun putting out all kinds of new leaves, twigs, and branches the next spring.

STAKING TREES

Young trees sometimes seem to be too thin to hold up the weight of their own branches and leaves. Being helpful, as most gardeners are, one or more stakes are pounded in the ground to help support the tree and keep it standing straight. Several things can go wrong at this stage of the tree's life:

- Stakes are pounded in very close to the tree, severing several roots.

- Three stakes and heavy guy wires are installed, totally immobilizing the entire tree

- One stake is driven in outside of the rootball and a wire is wrapped around the stake and the tree.

- Two stakes are driven on the downwind side of the tree with straps looped around the trunk

Why are these seemingly "helpful" steps a problem?

1. Young trees have a limited root ball—each root is important to carry water and

nutrients upward for the leaves and branches. Cutting the roots is like cutting the lifeline of the little tree. To re-grow roots in time to save the top is a difficult job; the job of just surviving the planting is plenty for any tree.

2. Wood in the tree grows stronger by waving and swaying in the breeze. Think of a broken arm—the arm is put in a cast so the bone can grow back together. When the cast is removed, the bone is fine but the muscles of the arm are weak from a month or two of immobility. If the rigid supports on a tree are left for more than one growing season, the new growth of wood above the supports will be strong from moving in the air. The trunk from the supports down will be much weaker. The first really strong wind that blows against the tree can snap the trunk right in two where the weak and strong wood meet.

3. Any material rubbing against the trunk can damage the bark. Wire does more than that. It can cut right through the outer bark and then sever the tissue that conducts water and nutrients to the upper tree and that takes the sugar to the roots for more growth. Within a few weeks a thin wire can cut right to the wood.

4. If you do have strong prevailing winds, the tree can be tilted a little into the wind but any tension downwind will just bend the tree further and further in that direction.

There is a purpose and method for successfully giving support to a young tree. Sometimes an area is plagued with constant wind or strong gusts coming from the same direction. A young tree hasn't a chance of being stable long enough to grow roots to keep it in the ground. Proper staking for a single growing season will give it the stability to grow those roots.

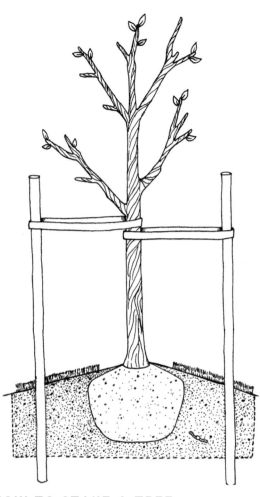

HOW TO STAKE A TREE

There are at least two methods of giving support without damage to any part of the new tree.

One is to pound short stakes into the ground four or more feet from the trunk. Two or three stakes will do the trick. You may need to round up a Boy Scout to remind you of proper tent staking protocol, but this is the same general idea: slant the stakes slightly away from the tree on the upwind side, or on three equal sides if the wind swirls a lot. Use a short length of old hose to protect the bark of the tree—run the cord, cable, rope, or whatever you are using through the hose and put the hose section against the trunk.

You can also place support close to the tree using long posts or stakes. These should be put into the ground at the same time the tree is planted. Jamming stakes down through the rootball as an afterthought will surely damage several roots. Put the two stakes perpendicular to the way the wind most often blows. (See diagram on page 39.) Use soft material or the "hose" protection to wrap around the tree. Old nylons (pantyhose) work well for this method. One full growing season, spring to spring or fall to fall, is as long as the support should remain on the tree.

IS IT A TREE OR A SHRUB?

Since both trees and shrubs are woody plants, the distinction is really in the eye of the planter. A 30-foot tall Giant Sequoia is pretty much a sure thing for the tree category. What about an 18-foot tall multi-stemmed Big Tooth Maple? Certainly a tree! Or a 15-foot tall, multi-stemmed Snowball Viburnam? How about a single-stemmed 15-foot Smoke Bush? Generally we can call a woody plant, single or multi-stem, that grows over 15 feet tall a tree. Shrubs and bushes usually grow less than 15 feet tall. You are probably already mentally listing the "Yeah, but," exceptions, aren't you? "Yeah-buts" include 3-foot tall Japanese maple trees, 20-foot tall Juniper bushes and 8-foot tall flowering cherry trees.

As for shrubs vs. bushes, "Pick your choose," as my brother used to say—a little shrub or a big bush—it doesn't really matter what you call it, as long as you plant it properly and take good care of it!

PLANTING SHRUBS

Whether deciduous or evergreen, shrubs can be planted in the fall. A proper planting hole is the same proportion as for trees: two to three times as wide as the root ball and just barely as deep as the root ball. The procedure is the same as well. Fall is more than just a good time for planting—it is an economical time for buying! End-of-season sales can save you 20, 30, 50 percent or more on the plants.

A fall without much precipitation means both the new and established shrubs (ones that have been growing two or more years) will need extra water until the soil freezes solid. Always check the soil moisture before you water, and then water slowly to allow the water to seep deeply into the soil. If soil is dry below two inches, it is time to water. Watering during an exceptionally dry winter should only be done on days when the temperature rises above freezing.

WINTER PROTECTION FOR NEEDLED EVERGREEN SHRUBS AND TREES

If you have new or established upright evergreen shrubs, like junipers or arborvitae, this is the time to consider wrapping them to keep the snow from bending down the branches. Without a wrap of some sort, these shrubs do a fair imitation of a half-peeled banana by the time spring has come. Regular heavy snowfall as well as snow sliding from a roof can cause the problem. Start near the trunk and tie the end of two-inch wide burlap to the shrub. The burlap can be purchased in roles at most nurseries and garden centers. Wrap the shrub in a spiral pattern with the strips of burlap 4 to 8 inches apart until you get to the top of the shrub and tie off the end. Remove the wrap once the likelihood of a major snow storm has passed.

BROADLEAF EVERGREENS

For broadleaf evergreens like Boxwood, Laurels,

Oregon Grape, or Euonymous, a spray of an anti-desiccant will reduce the number of leaves that turn whitish and brittle from the cold of winter. This product reduces the amount of water leaves lose from their exposed surfaces and should be sprayed on both the top and bottom sides of the leaves. Wait until the daytime temperatures are around 45°F before you spray.

Taller pine, spruce, and fir trees can usually just have the snow bounced or brushed from their branches, and they will be fine. Don't pound forcefully though—those cold brittle branches break more easily in the winter than when they are warm and flexible during the other seasons.

DECIDUOUS TREES

There are a couple of ways to help deciduous trees get through the winter in good condition. This first procedure is particularly important for young trees that have been in the garden for less than five years. Wrap the exposed trunk with white wrap (or paint with white paint) from the lowest branch on down to the ground. When temperatures reach above 40 degrees during a warm winter day, bark heats up and sap begins to thin and starts to flow. Then the night temperatures drop, sometimes as much as 50 degrees. It is certainly below freezing and may even end up below zero and the sap freezes. When the watery sap freezes it swells and that causes little cells in the bark to burst from the swelling. It isn't a visible damage, and so it doesn't show up until next spring when the tree is trying to conduct water and nutrients up from the roots. Just like a broken water pipe, the burst cells can't get the fluid up to where it is needed and bark begins to die and split, exposing bare wood.

White tree wrap reflects the sunlight, keeping the bark from warming and the sap from starting to flow. Begin at the bottom of the trunk and wrap with overlapping layers upwards until the first branch is reached. Then tie off the wrap so it won't unwind. You can get the same protection for the bark by painting the tree with white latex paint that has been mixed half and half with water.

Remove the wrap when the trees begin to grow in the spring. No need to try to remove the paint. As the bark on the tree grows it will just peel and wear away.

WATERING BEFORE WINTER

It's very important to water trees and shrubs well before the winter sets in to help them stay healthy throughout the winter. A general rule is to apply ten gallons of water for each diameter inch of the tree. For example, a three-inch diameter tree will need thirty gallons. This water should be evenly distributed around the drip line. Depending on your soil type, you may need to space this watering over hours or even days. If the warm weather of autumn stretches out through November, your trees and shrubs may need a second deep watering. Young plants might even need water in December or January—check the soil for moisture if it thaws out.

Flowers in the Fall

ANNUAL VS. PERENNIAL VS. BIENNIAL

For a plant to be classified as an annual, it needs to germinate from a seed, produce a flower, which then produces seed. After seed has been produced, the plant dies. All of this takes place during a single growing season.

It's difficult to keep the terms annual and perennial straight. Winter usually kills annuals if they are left outside after temperatures drop much below 30 degrees. Winter usually kills perennials in proportion to how much money you paid for them. However, the word *perennial* does mean that they should return in the garden for several years.

Perennials are defined as plants that continue to grow for more than two seasons. Each year after the plant becomes mature, it will produce flowers, set seed, and continue for repeated years. Some plants that are termed perennials in a warm area would be grown as annuals in a colder climate.

Perennials get their sometimes-only-honorary designation from the theory that they do stay growing in the garden for years and years and get prettier and prettier with hardly any effort on your part. As theories go, this is hardly a useful one. Don't get pushed into believing perennials are the supreme solution for a continually blooming beautiful garden. But that's another story. (See summer care of perennials, page 122.)

Before and after their bloom period, perennials are just green leaves and stems (which is most of the year for many perennials). My garden is mostly green leaves, stems, and trees, and I love it that way! The textures, the subtle shades of green, the fleeting, ephemeral glimpses of color—that's my little piece of heaven.

Between annual and perennial are the plants designated as biennial. "Bi" means two, as in bi-cycle meaning two-wheeled transportation. A biennial, then, is a plant that takes two years to complete its life cycle. It grows from seed to plant the first year. During the second growing season, it grows flowers, sets seed, and dies. Examples of biennials are

Foxglove, Sweet William, and most Hollyhocks. If you buy one of these flowers in its first year, you may be disappointed by not having flowers at all. Just hang on—the next year is when the flowers show up. But if you buy them in full flower, that's it—no flowers the next year, because the plant died over the winter.

If you let the plant go on to form seeds after the flowers finish blooming, the seeds might germinate and you will have several little plants that form their leaves next year. No flowers—remember, they will come the year after that. To keep a patch of these biennials in flower year after year just plant both the leaf, or rosette, stage and one that is blooming next to each other. One will form seeds to grow into the leafy form the next year while the other is waiting as a rosette to bloom the following year. Kind of tricky, but it will make the flower patch seem like the same flowers keep coming back year after year.

PLANTING PERENNIALS

Fall is a wonderful time to plant perennials. Nice cool air with warm soil gives the plants a chance to get their roots established without the stress of intense sun and high temperatures. Even the perennials that "die" back to the ground each year have plenty of cool sunny days to settle in. These herbaceous perennials can cause near stoppage of the heart for gardeners when the plants do their disappearing act for the winter. Actually it isn't so much the disappearing part that is anxiety producing; it's the very, very long delay before reappearing in the spring that can do you in. Some perennials are so slow to emerge that you only know that they are alive by digging into them with damaging results. And why were you digging there in the first place? You were just trying to fill the disappointing gap they left created by their apparent death—the news of which death, it turns out, was greatly exaggerated.

ANNUALS IN THE FALL

If you are going to coax every last blossom out of your annuals during the growing season, early September is the time to give them their final dose of fertilizer. Deadheading will prolong their last gasp of color as well. If a killing frost is late in coming, flowers may last until Halloween, except at higher elevations, where that late of a frost is a rarity.

Deadheading is not on the trail after Jerry Garcia, nor a sadistic way to decapitate weeds. When an individual flower is finished blooming and the petals are all dried up, pruners or scissors are used to clip off the dead head or blossom of the flower. For the neatest, tidiest looking plant, follow the stem that held the flower down to where you find the first green leaf and cut just above that leaf.

The plant cannot continue to put energy into ripening seeds because you just removed the part that would have become seeds. Foiled at completing the reproduction cycle, most plants once again start to set flower buds. Annual flowering plants keep up the production for as long as they are alive and healthy.

TO CLEAN UP OR NOT TO CLEAN UP IN THE ANNUAL FLOWER GARDEN— THAT IS THE QUESTION

The process of deadheading flowers differs from cutting off or pulling up entire plants during the end-of-season cleanup in the garden. That final cleanup does not lead to more flowers—it leads to the compost pile. You can run and put off getting the flower garden cleaned up in the late fall, but you can't hide. Okay, so you can hide in the house during the winter, but the mess will still be out there come springtime.

So is it better to do cleanup in the fall? The answer depends on who you ask.

I have gardening friends who enjoy traveling during the fall months and use Labor Day weekend to both labor and end their gardens. Since most weekends and some full weeks will find them off enjoying one thing or another, they completely clean out all of their garden spaces during the three-day holiday.

At some point you must decide, "Is it now?" or "Will it be spring?" Sometimes circumstances dictate which it will be. Either way, you have the final say for your garden. You could really flip a coin to decide on the time for garden cleanup, since both fall and next spring have their devotees. And both choices have their advantages and disadvantages. The following breakdown may help you decide what is best for you and *your* garden:

AUTUMN CLEAN UP

- No extra housing for insects over the winter.
- A neat and tidy look all fall (If you start early enough—just before the snow flies won't give you much time to admire the "neat and tidy.")
- Plenty of material for the compost pile or a municipal green recycling bin
- Places that need more organic matter are easily spotted.
- Bulbs for spring blooms are more easily planted.

SPRING CLEAN UP

- You don't have to do the work yet!
- Seeds on many of the plants make for happy birds.

- The dry stems and leaves make for lovely winter interest in the garden. (I personally think that is fooey—the only "winter interest" I want to see in the winter garden is deep snow starting in November and getting deeper every week until it melts March first on the dot.)

- Flowers that reseed themselves get every chance to do their reseeding.

So, again, pick your choose. This is a chore that really needs to be done in one season or the other. When did you say your vacation was? There, that's the perfect time NOT to do the work. Unless you have become a *gardener*—then the work is a vacation and probably therapy to boot!

TO CLEAN UP OR NOT IN THE PERENNIAL GARDEN

Here comes decision time again—to cut back or not cut back perennials, that is the question. And again, proponents are found on both sides of the issue.

The arguments are nearly the same as with annuals. In areas with wet winters or long periods of snow covering the ground, the plant residue can cause real problems. Because the plant remains bogged down, it becomes soggy around the top, or crown, of the perennials, and this can set up conditions for diseases to attack, and even kill, the plant. That doesn't bother annuals, because they have gone to plant heaven already.

It's your decision—flip a coin if you want. How much did you spend on those perennials? Not trying to influence your decision in any way, though!

BULBS IN THE FALL

Gardeners are always dreaming of the garden to come, and this time of year that garden is found in the contemplation of what is to come next spring. The action that fulfills this dream is planting bulbs— dozens and dozens of bulbs. Hundreds, if that is possible considering space and, let's face it, money. Even a tight budget might have a little loose change for a couple of bulbs. Keep in mind the Arabic saying, "If a man has but two nickels, he should buy bread with one and a hyacinth with the other."

To get color that will really get your attention when spring arrives, bulbs should be planted in groups rather than singly. For example, crocus show up best in groups of roughly 15 or 20 per square foot. Be sure to have them up close to the sidewalk or near the front door where people will often walk by. They are lovely for such a short time and are really so small in size that one or two planted in an out-of-the-way spot could come into bloom and be gone before you ever noticed them.

Daffodils are the bulbs of choice for anyone who lives in an area considered the "lunchroom" by roaming deer. Deer won't eat them at all. That is true about alliums as well—known as ornamental onions, some of these flashy flowers can stand 4 feet tall while other varieties have balls made up of little individual flowers that can grow up to a foot across.

Tulips come in nearly all colors of the rainbow and stand from 3 inches to 3 feet tall depending on the variety. Do remember, though, that tulips are deer candy.

Spring fragrance wouldn't be complete without some of the jewel-colored hyacinths. They tend to decline in blooms after the second year, so I recommend planting at least two new clusters of at least three bulbs every year.

It is preferable to plant bulbs sometime toward the end of September through October. They

should go in pointy side up and into a hole three times as deep as the bulb is wide. For good root growth, the hole should also be at least twice as wide as the bulb. Should the season get away from you, it is possible to plant bulbs in a snowstorm or after scraping six inches of snow from the garden bed. And you can chip away at the first inch of frozen soil to find the open soil below to get those last few bulbs planted. (Just guess how I know these to be successful methods!)

Mulch

"MULCH" ADO ABOUT NOTHING—EXCEPT IN THE GARDEN

Mulching is a very simple, beneficial, and eye-catching practice to use in the garden. Often the terms "mulch" and "compost" are used interchangeably, but

are they really the same? No! Mulch is any material that is placed over the soil in a garden. Compost is the end result of the decomposition of organic matter that is then added to soil as a soil amendment. Compost can be used as mulch, but mulch is not necessarily compost.

Mulching both vegetable gardens and flower beds can be a great time-saving tactic for a variety of reasons:

- Keeps the soil moist and reduces the need for constant watering.
- Helps maintain an even soil temperature.
- Prevents and hinders the growth of weeds.
- Organic mulch enriches the soil by slowly releasing nitrogen and nutrients.
- Gives flower beds a finished and professional look.
- Reduces compaction of the soil from foot traffic and storms.
- Allows access to the garden even when damp—no muddy feet.
- Keeps fruits and vegetables clean and off the ground.

Mulches can either be organic or inorganic. Both organic and inorganic mulches have numerous benefits.

You have many choices of **organic** mulches, from grass clippings to straw, wood chips to cocoa bean hulls. Some smell good, some are a rich dark brown, and some are great because they are free! Whichever organic mulch you choose, it will slowly decompose and help keep the soil loose which improves root growth, improves the water-holding capacity of the soil, and becomes a great source of plant nutrients.

Inorganic mulch has a place in the landscape as well but can be more permanent and difficult to

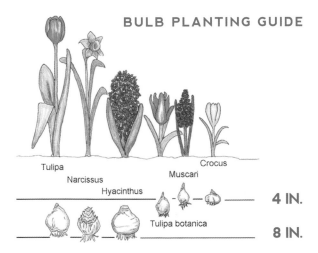

BULB PLANTING GUIDE

Tulipa
Narcissus
Hyacinthus
Muscari
Crocus

4 IN.

Tulipa botanica

8 IN.

remove. Examples can be gravel, stones, brick chips, landscape fabric, or plastic sheeting. A fairly new product on the market is a rubber mulch made from recycled tires! These mulches do have many of the same helpful characteristics of organic mulch but lack their soil-improving qualities.

Mulch materials can be found in your own yard and home. If you take a newspaper, you are having potential garden mulch delivered right to your door! A thick layer of six to seven sheets of newsprint works well as a mulch. Remember to get the newspaper wet before laying it out in the garden—it doesn't blow away when it's wet! Since most newspapers have vegetable-based inks, there's no need to worry about damage to the environment. For example, smell a newspaper. If it smells a little like rotten eggs, it's probably printed using soy-based ink. Finish reading the paper first, of course, and then take it outside and use it as a mulch.

Lawn clippings make excellent mulch, particularly for vegetable gardens, as long as you haven't used dandelion-type weed killers on the lawn. Many people put down newspaper between the garden rows and then add the grass clippings on top. Alone, the clippings can be easily spread around even small plants. Too thick a layer of grass clippings will rot, and things that rot stink, so add a thin layer, no more than 2 or 3 inches, at a time.

Leaves are another great mulch material easily found in large quantities. Leaves can be chopped into smaller pieces by running over them a couple of times with your lawn mower. Store them in piles or plastic bags through the fall and winter. The leaves can then be brought out in the summer and added to the garden. Hay and straw can work well in a vegetable garden, although they may harbor weed seeds.

Rich, dark compost makes a beautiful top-dressing or mulch in gardens and flower beds. In the fall, this can be turned under to improve the soil and add a variety of nutrients.

Bark chips and composted bark mulch are available either packaged or loose at garden centers. These will also eventually break down and improve the soil. The finer the chips or bark, the sooner it will decompose and more will need to be added.

In a garden that contains raised beds, a permanent mulch of pea gravel works well in the areas between the boxes. Rock mulch absorbs heat during the day and releases the heat at night. This can cause some extra water loss but will also help keep plants warm during cool nights. Light-colored materials will reflect sunlight and cause the temperature around the plants to be warmer.

Black plastic is not recommended as a mulch material for landscape plants. Plastic will help control most weeds all righty dighty and does conserve water, but it does not allow water, nutrients, and air to move freely to the soil below. And when it starts to break up (oh, yes, it will), it will drive you to distraction trying to gather up all the tattered pieces. And

to add to the disadvantages, plants often develop a very shallow root system under the plastic that is more subject to damage during severe drought or cold weather. Clear or black plastic can be used to raise the soil temperature on sunny days—a blessing to those crops that need the extra heat.

Allow the soil to warm up in the spring before applying mulch so intentionally planted seeds will germinate well and perennials will begin to grow. Many mulches provide an insulating barrier between the soil and air, so a soil that has been mulched will be cooler in the summer than surrounding bare soil. Because of this insulation, mulched soils cool down more slowly in the fall and warm up more slowly in the spring.

Fall mulching over perennial beds, around roses, and in a strawberry bed is best done after the soil has frozen in the late fall/early winter. The purpose of mulch in these areas is to keep the soil cold through the winter—not to tuck the plants into a cozy warmer bed. During a warm spell on a winter day, the soil may begin to thaw out a little. Then it will freeze again when the temperatures drop at night. This alternating freeze-thaw cycle causes a phenomenon called "heaving." The heaving process can lift plants right out of the soil, exposing tender roots to the dry, freezing air.

In order to obtain the maximum benefits of using organic mulch, the layer should be between 2 to 4 inches thick after it settles. Coarse mulch can help prevent weeds from sprouting more than fine mulch unless the fine mulch is 3 or 4 inches deep. Before adding the mulch, remove any weeds that are in the area and give the soil a thorough soaking. Mulch should be placed on top of the soil and not mixed into the soil as mixing can inhibit plant growth or

Bonus Box: To eliminate grass around the base of a tree without the need to dig, use a thick layer of old newspapers or a piece of cardboard directly on the grass. Then top with any attractive organic mulch.

damage fragile roots.

Mulching around trees and shrubs is a good way to reduce landscape maintenance and keeps plants healthy. If trees and shrubs are grown in a lawn area, damage often occurs to the bark resulting in either "mower-itis" or "string-trimmer disease." Both of these conditions result from trying to get that last blade of grass that is up against a tree trunk. Cutting through the thin living layer just below the outer bark causes the tissue that moves water up the tree and the food down from the leaves to be damaged. If the damage is all the way around the trunk the tree usually dies. It may be a slow, painful death over a few years, but it will eventually succumb to the wound. To eliminate this problem, remove the lawn in a circle at least 3 feet out from the tree trunk, and replace the lawn with coarse mulch such as shredded bark. Mulching can be done at planting time. It can also be done around established trees. Just spread a deep layer of mulch right over the existing grass. It is important to pull back the mulch 1 to 2 inches from around the base of the tree to prevent bark decay. Before long, the shade of the mulch will smother the grass. Any grass that pokes its head through can be pulled fairly easily.

Some gardeners feel that if some mulch is good, more mulch is better. However, the mulch layer can become too deep. Mulch that is too deep results in a situation where the roots are growing in the mulch and not in the soil. These shallow roots are apt to dry out more during hot weather and get damaged by any activity around the tree.

Think back to the last time you walked through a forest. Pine needles, leaves, dead plant material, rotten wood, and other debris covered the forest floor. This is nature's mulch. You can learn from this and create the same conditions found in nature right in your own yard. Growing your own great mulch will just become a regular part of your gardening pleasure.

FINAL THOUGHTS OF THE SEASON

Just a final thought for the season—have you noticed that the muscles used to rake leaves are not used for any other motion the human body makes? No matter how fit or in shape you are, that first or third or seventeenth or forty-third time you spend four hours raking, there are going to be muscles in your back screaming at you: "What do you mean? We're going to do this again? Can't you hire somebody else to wage war with these leaves? You're going to regret this! You can't buy a big enough heating pad to keep me quiet."

About the time the knots are releasing from those aching raking muscles, other muscles just down the back start yelling "A snow shovel? I thought we bought a snow blower last year. Did that weatherman say 15 inches of snow by morning? Oh, you're going to regret this!"

December, January, and February

DECEMBER, JANUARY, AND FEBRUARY

MINI GLOSSARY

Dormant season	Time when plants are not actively growing.
Standard tree	One that reaches full size; for apples that is 30–40 feet tall; Blue spruce is 60+ feet tall and 25–30 feet across.
Dwarf tree	Growth is from 6 to 20 feet tall, depending on the kind of tree.

CLOSING DOWN THE TOOL SHED

As the end of November draws the curtains and starts the process of bedding down the garden for the winter, very few chores are left remaining outside in the garden. Rounding up (ahem, finding) all the tools used in various endeavors is one that shouldn't be neglected. There is always the danger that a hoe or rake might sneak under your foot and throw you on your head. And next spring you will want to be ready for all things bright and gardening.

Basic tools for the garden like shovels, trowels, and rakes need the soil knocked off them. Scrubbing a little with steel wool or a kitchen scrubby pad and soap and water should take care of the stubborn soil in the crevices. A light spray or wipe down with oil will keep the working end of the tools in tip-top shape for next year's most excellent garden.

Your hands—and the hands of any helpers you get to "volunteer"—will also be relieved if you spend just a little time on the tool handles. I've been told that the handles of my tools would need very little care if they spent more time upright in the tool closet and less time waiting in the soil/flower bed/herb patch with their handle on the ground or propped up against the tree. The tools were probably put down "just for a second" when I spotted yet another patch of Field Bindweed peaking out from under a rose-bush on the other side of the garden.

To give the handles the care they deserve, first scrape or scrub the soil off of the wood—or plastic, or metal. For the wooden handles, a light pass or two with fine-grained sandpaper will remove most of the potential slivers. Give them a light rub with an old rag moistened with some boiled Linseed oil, and they're ready to put away for the winter. You can stop at the scrape and scrub part for metal or plastic handles.

For tools that are already in good shape (that means were not left out in the garden way too often) use a technique that only requires a bucket of sand and some used motor oil. Pour about a cup of used oil into the bucket of sand and mix well. After you knock off most of the dried soil, push your cleaned tools, business end only, up and down in the sand a few times. The grit of the sand in addition to the tiny metal particles in the oil will buff the last of the lingering soil particles away. In addition, the oil supplies a nice protection from the moisture during the winter, banishing the possibility of any rust deposits on the tools.

If November and the first part of December have been exceptionally dry, then any new plants in the garden probably need some additional water. Check the soil first, and if it is moist, forget about it. However, dry soil should be watered slowly around the entire tree, shrub, or perennial, but not right up against the stem. If the soil is already frozen, wait a day when the temperature rises above freezing.

Hoses should be drained, coiled, and put away before the water in them freezes solid. Ho boy, is it ever impossible to coil a frozen hose! I've tried. On a warmish day when the temperature gets into the forties, I stretch my hose (after unscrewing it from the faucet) down my driveway. There is just enough of an incline for the water to drain out completely. I keep the hose close to the front of the tool closet, though. Just in case I do need to drag it out again during a dry fall or winter to give the trees or new plants a late season drink.

Leaves continue to fall from some trees well into December, and if a snowstorm doesn't beat you to the punch and cover them, they should be raked off the lawn. Matted lawn under matted leaves can lead to conditions that not only make your lawn look scroungy in the spring, but also might cause some patches of grass to die out entirely.

WINTERIZING THE LAWN

If snow is a little late in coming, you may find that you have some bonus time to finish up projects that either you didn't get to or that need doing again. Perhaps those last, lingering leaves flutter to the ground after the rakes have been stored away for the winter. If so, take a few minutes before the snow flies, get the rake one more time and clean up any debris that is still on the lawn.

Enjoying Seasonal Plants

While the outside gardening chores wind down by November, a gardener's twitching fingers move toward plants, kept in the house. Ivy, philodendron, spider plants and their house-bound friends receive all the attention that was lacking during the outside growing season. Just about the time they think they

are actually the center of your gardening universe, along come those flash-in-the-pan upstart holiday plants!

Many of our favorite seasonal plants can be treated as lovely annuals. That means (as with marigolds and petunias) these plants have a limited life expectancy, and so there should be little guilt associated with sending them on to the great compost pile of life. It is perfectly reasonable and permissible to toss the plants out when the Christmas decorations come down or when the poinsettia loses most of its leaves—whichever comes first.

POINSETTIA

Poinsettias, once tall lanky wild flowers of Mexico, now come in a startling array of sizes and, honestly, unnatural colors. And just in case you ever wondered, these seasonal lovelies don't grow leaves that automatically sparkle with layers of glitter either. Joel Poinsett, ambassador to Mexico in the early 1800s, brought the plant home to South Carolina and the tinkering began.

Poinsettias (pronounced poin-set-uh OR poin-set-ee-uh, take your pick) have become the poster

flower for the red and green season—except when they are purple or blue. Folks who fiddle with cross-breeding poinsettias have actually developed varieties that do have different colored leaves. There can be cream, pink, white, speckled, mauve, almost burgundy, nearly yellow, streaked, and nearly black-red. My favorite is Jingle Bells—a bright true red with pink speckles. The purple, blue, and turquoise leaves are painted to reach that end of the rainbow. All of the bright colors are specialized leaves called "bracts," whether painted or natural. The actual flower of the poinsettia is the little yellow button in the center.

There are a few things you can do to keep a poinsettia looking perky and healthy while you showcase its seasonal color:

1. Protect the plant from blasts of cold air—like when you leave the heated store and slog through 22 degrees of sleet and snow to get to your car. Have the clerk put the pot in a bag, preferably paper, and then cover the top of the plant with a second bag. The stop to buy the poinsettia should be the last one on your buying list. Leaving the poinsettia in a cold car while you are trying once again to find the perfect gift for Uncle Ken is going to set the plant up for a shortened life. It will look fine when you get it home but within a day or so the leaves will begin to curl from the edges, start to dry, and then fall off. All of the leaves will probably do this. If you put the plant really close to the front door where the arctic blast from outside blows in, the leaves will do the same thing.

2. Protect the plant from blasts of warm air, like the warm air that comes from a heating duct. Poinsettias like warmer temperatures, but only if they are combined with humidity of 50 percent or higher. Forced air heating usually results in humidity levels of less than 5 percent.

3. Remove the plastic or foil "sleeve" that covers the pot. Should it really look better to you with the sleeve on, poke a few holes in the bottom of the covering to let excess water drain into a saucer (plant type, not cup-and-saucer type, unless of course that is the only kind of saucer you have. I'm sure the poinsettia would be honored to sit on Great Aunt Teddie's hand-painted porcelain saucer).

4. Keep the soil just moist—you can tell if it needs watering by picking up the pot. If it feels like it's full of packing peanuts and weighs about half an ounce, it needs water. You could also use the pokey-finger method—if you poke your finger into the soil and it's dry past the first joint, it's time to water.

5. If you're using the poinsettia for only short seasonal display, it will be gorgeous anywhere in your home. If you want to take the challenge of keeping it as a long-lasting houseplant, it should be in a spot with good light, near a window.

AMARYLLIS

An amaryllis is a large bulb that makes its appearance during the holidays. This is the stately queen of the seasonal plants. The flower stalk, topped by four enormous trumpet-shaped flowers, can often be 2 feet tall. Very large bulbs may even send up two or three of the flower stalks producing a spectacular display of eight or even twelve trumpets blooming at the same time. Making this display even more breathtaking are the colors that are found in the different varieties. Glorious red, brilliant white, pink, white with pink striping, apricot, and white with red

stripes really make this a gorgeous centerpiece for any seasonal display.

You need to be quite devoted to the bulb to keep it as an unusual house plant after it finishes flowering. If you don't have place for a bulb that now has several three-foot-long, strap-like leaves, just send it to the ever-ready compost pile or green waste bin. Optimism, foolish or otherwise, is encouraged by instructions included in most amaryllis boxes. "Keep the bulb alive and growing with its large straplike leaves through an entire growing season until next fall and you too can bring it back into flower by Christmas!"

I know people that actually pull off that optimistic gardening endeavor—for every one of them I also know roughly thousands who find they have only large, straplike leaves to show for their long drawn out effort. So, take your choice!

CHRISTMAS CACTUS

Christmas cactus (sometimes called Easter or Thanksgiving cactus) can almost become a member of the family because it lives so long. No seasonal flash in the pan, this one. Once you find the spot it loves, it will bloom its little heart out for years to come. That perfect spot has indirect light from a window, cool night time temperatures, and no drafts—either cold or warm.

Some folks like to keep the cactus in a back bedroom until it comes into flower and then move it out to show off for visitors. This works well if you remember to keep the same side of the plant toward the window as it was when it was in the bedroom. The flower buds turn towards the light and can pop their little heads off, turning to face a window or light, shining on the other side of the plant!

The Christmas cactus is not a desert cactus but a plant whose relatives live in jungles. They are most often found up in the trees in a crevice or crotch of large branches. Conditions in the trees boast consistent moisture and filtered light. This is the condition you want to recreate to keep the Christmas cactus happy. The potting soil should be kept just moist

during the blooming period and then left to dry out just a little between waterings during the resting period. Don't be too anxious to put the little plant into a larger pot—they do their best when slightly pot-bound. The only signal to move on up to a larger pot is either no blooms for an entire year or a continual battle to keep it from toppling over because it is top heavy.

PAPERWHITE NARCISSUS

Paperwhite Narcissus usually makea its appearance around the holiday season. Paperwhite bulbs can be grown without soil, just with rocks in the container. You need a container with NO drainage since the water level needs to stay just below the top of the rocks. Put a layer of rocks in the container and set the bulb on the rocks. Make the bulb deep enough so you can add rocks to cover about ⅓ of the bulb and bring the rocks up to about an inch from the top of the pot. Pour water into the container, stopping just below the top of the rocks. Keep the water at this level through the growing period. When they are forced into bloom as a seasonal houseplant and the flowers dry up, it's into the compost pile with them. The energy expended for display of flowers doesn't leave them enough reserve to bloom again

Paperwhites usually become lanky and top heavy if left to their own devices. You can just keep propping them up or tying them together or leaning them against the wall or stack of books. A great deal of bright sunlight slows the long skinny growth a little. If you don't find math and details too daunting, you may want to try this addition to their water, whether in soil or the rocks:

Use alcohol, regular rubbing or good ol' drinking alcohol. If you share your own drink with the paperwhites, they prefer the clear alcohol—vodka, gin, or the like. And don't use wine, white or otherwise. Too much sugar and mold will grow, causing quite a literal stink. Somewhere on the bottle you will find the percentage of alcohol in the liquid. For instance, rubbing alcohol is usually 70 percent alcohol. Divide that number by 5 and subtract 1 from the answer. Therefore: $70 \div 5 = 14$, $14 - 1 = 13$.

The result gives you the parts of water per one part alcohol. So mix a pitcher of 13 tablespoons of water and add 1 tablespoon of alcohol and use it to water your paperwhites. Just like your mom used to say, "It will stunt your (their) growth!" Paperwhites will stay stockier and be less likely to tip over or bend nearly in half from the weight of the blossoms.

Be very careful to discard any extra alcohol solution, especially if you use rubbing alcohol, as it is harmful to take internally. Mix up a fresh batch each time you need to water, or mark the container very visibly that it is not for drinking.

Oh, and before you rush right out and buy a dozen bulbs to force for your holiday decorations, you better find some already blooming and take a sniff. I like the fragrance—it reminds me of spring. However, a good many folks seem to think it is more reminiscent of socks long over due for a good washing. And even if you do enjoy the smell, they are so potent that one or two will "perfume" an entire room.

CHRISTMAS TREES

Christmas trees, not usually thought of as annuals, become disposable annuals after the Christmas season. Handy-dandy artificial trees have pushed cut trees into second place in the Christmas decoration race. But as a nostalgic and even renewable source of holiday cheer, I just don't think you can beat a "real" Christmas tree. My fondest memories of Christmas tree hunting are of my dad, mom, brother, and I trudging through at least ankle-deep snow with the wind whipping the snow between the trees and into our faces. Mom would say, "No, the top isn't right" for the twentieth time, in the fifth tree lot. Logic tells me that it couldn't have been snowing and blowing every time we went to choose a tree, but it's hard to recollect any sunny days.

Our (let that read Mom's) perfect tree was always a Balsam Fir, very recently cut, with a perfect top. The perfect top had only one—no double tops—straight, no more than 8-inch long tip above the first whorl of branches. *Then* the rest of the branches needed to be perfectly spaced so the lead icicles could hang down without hitting the next tier of branches. Dad was in charge of cutting off the bottom of the tree so it could fit in the stand and then wrapping and clipping the lights onto the branches. The rest of us sat across the room and directed the placement of the individual light bulbs. Sometimes there were too many red ones on one side or the other. Sometimes there was only one yellow one showing, so dad had to unscrew one from the backside of the tree to switch out with one of the blue ones on the front side.

After the lights came the ornaments. When we got to be a certain age, we were allowed to hang a few ornaments. They were all very delicate glass and had been handed down to Mom from her mother and grandmother. Then came the icicles. Each one hung on a single needle and every needle had its lead icicle. Yes, lead! Not those coated plastic things that cling to everything and nearly follow you across the room because of static electricity. The icicles were also removed one icicle at a time and stored for the next Christmas in a Janet Russell Candy Box. I still have those icicles in that box, and they get lovingly draped individually over single needles every year resulting in the entire tree looking like it has been encased in silver ice.

Now, let me tell you how hard it is to find the right kind of cut tree these days. First, wild-cut Balsam and sub-alpine firs are no longer available. Only plantation-grown trees are sold in the Christmas tree lots. Folks have been convinced that the bushy full symmetrical Grand or Noble fir is the Christmas standard. So I usually have to resort to buying one of the 12-foot giants that are usually sold to businesses that need a very tall, sparse tree. Then I cut off the top 5 feet or so and that top is my tree!

The most common trees sold for Christmas are fir, with their flat, friendly needles. Next in popularity is the pine; pretty pokey but not too bad. Last—way last—on the list is a spruce. I've talked to a few people who tried a spruce Christmas tree, just like I did . . . once. It's like decorating an angry porcupine with all its quills up.

A cut tree of any kind needs a fresh cut taken on the trunk before it is set in a stand that holds water. Many tree lots still offer to cut the end of the tree for you (take them up on the service), but if it is more than a half hour before you can get the tree home and into a bucket of water, it will still need another inch or so cut off the trunk. In that much time, sap begins to clog the vessels that would have taken up water to keep the tree fresh throughout the season.

When I sold Christmas trees with Redwood Nursery, there was a certain percentage of the trees that would have a problem staying fresh. We used a technical horticultural phrase for this problem— *they were toast!* Some stress at the field or during transportation damaged the tree so thoroughly that it would start to dry and drop needles within a day or two of being decorated. Over the many, many years of selling the freshest trees that could be found, the percentage of trees that were toast was about 1 percent of the total number of the trees we sold. That percentage stayed pretty constant for every kind of spruce, pine, or fir. Only the sheared Douglas Fir trees seemed to have a few more that were disappointedly premature toast.

> **Bonus Box:** How to tell what type of needled evergreen trees you have:
>
> **F** Fir needles are flat and friendly.
>
> **P** Pine needles come in pokey packets or pairs.
>
> **S** Spruce needles are sharp and spiny squares.

To keep your tree from becoming "toast," a water stand is a must. And the water level should never drop below the cut end of the trunk. An anti-desiccant (known by some descriptive name like "Wilt-Pruf"), the same product used to winterize broadleaf evergreen plants outside, can help reduce water loss through the evergreen needles inside. Keep the tree outside for the spraying, let it dry, and then decorate as usual. There is an added benefit to this treatment because it also acts as a fire retardant.

Planning, Dreaming, and Scheming

CATALOGS

This is the most wonderful time of the year in the heart of a gardener. Around the first of January, the mail delivery starts the little gears just a-turning in a gardener's dreams. Seed and plant catalogs start to arrive! Oh, the delight of turning the page to find the very red corn and purple carrots you've been reading about pictured right there on the "Unusual Vegetables" page!

And even better, there are pictures of the garden just like the one you have! Well, maybe not *exactly* like yours. The one in the catalog doesn't have weeds or bare spots or weeds or half dead roses or weeds or yellow leaves or weeds or jagged edges around the lawn or a big blank space where the water feature will go or holes where the dog dug up the dahlias or weeds or tunnels and mounds where the gopher devoured the roots of the cherry tree. But other than that, it is exactly what you see when you look out your back door. (Well, it could be like that, and for now, that is *precisely* what you envision!)

Nearly every company that sells seeds or plant material now makes available an electronic version of the Winter Doldrums-Chasing Catalog. But it just isn't the same. Even with my laptop, the experience is muted—probably because the feet-propped-up-half-reclining-while-sipping-a-warm-beverage pose isn't very practical for gazing at the online version of a catalog. And even my trusty Mac has its limits when it comes to tolerance of cocoa spills.

"Hello, my name is Joy, and I am a hard-copy catalog addict" (See Favorite List, page 144.)

That admitted and out of the way, let me counsel you to consider using the catalogs—paper or electronic—as mostly a list factory for things you want to find at your local nursery or garden center. The stacks and stacks and stacks of catalogs found in boxes or, well, stacks of boxes, around my home are really for reference only. The first run-through of all the catalogs usually results in a shopping total that roughly equals more than you paid for your first car. Not to panic! This is the list from which you cull the *"I didn't really think that would grow here anyway"* rejects. Then the *"nearly like something else that died in the garden two years running"* part of the list drops out. Before you know it, you're back to just a little over what you spent the year before. Well, there were some new varieties of tomatoes that were begging to be let loose in your garden, so a teeny increase is understandable.

There are only two catalogs from which I have actually placed an order in the last twenty years. And, that was only *after* searching all my favorite local nursery haunts unsuccessfully for a particular plant and a specific packet of seeds. Local buying—after national dreaming—puts you ahead in every way thinkable. In the quest for THE garden of the coming year, take every advantage you can: locally, there are no shipping charges; no substitution variety of a dubious nature because your requested variety was no longer in stock; and no mostly dead, bedraggled plants that just spent the last twenty-four hours of their life stranded in a delivery truck broken down halfway across Kansas.

Cut out pictures from the catalogs and create a folder of "annuals," "perennials," "shrubs," and "trees." Then when you go to the local nursery, you can show the nursery folks what you have in mind. With their knowledge of your particular growing area, they can help you weed (sorry—couldn't help myself there) out the plants that just won't do well. They can also point out plants with the same characteristics you are after and that are very well-adapted to your garden conditions.

You will find nursery professionals especially eager to help you during this time of the year. They would much rather talk plants than wash another shelf or clean out another fish tank. By March and April, they will be so busy that they may only be able to spare two minutes for your questions.

PLANNING FOR TREES

Spring may be a great time to *plant* trees and shrubs, but *now* is the time to decide what you want and where it will grow. Waiting until you get to the nursery to decide will find you answering the siren call of a standard apple tree and a gorgeous Purple Beech and the most perfectly-shaped Blue Spruce you've ever seen. What's wrong with that, you ask? If you only have a small back yard, maybe 50 by 75 feet, those three trees alone will fill the entire area and the larger portion of three neighboring yards as well.

Planning during these winter months will get you a list including a dwarf apple tree, a dwarf Blue Spruce and a columnar (narrow) Purple Beech. *And* your backyard that would *still* be roomy enough for a vegetable garden, a small lawn, roses, and place for the kids to play alongside a nice deck. Yes, *really!*

Winter Bits and Pieces

SNOW PROBLEMS FOR TREES AND SHRUBS

Snow poses a problem for the evergreen trees out in the garden. When the snow sticks and begins to pile on the branches, it can get so heavy that the branches split or break right off. The break is almost always jagged and the only thing that can be done is to use a saw and make a clean, proper cut at the base of the limb.

Evergreen shrubs face damage from the snow too. Branches are weighted down but are limber enough to just give with the pressure. Next spring,

> **High on a Mountain Tip:** Winter mulching can protect perennials from dying during the winter. Wait until the ground freezes and add mulch for some extra protection. Deep snow is actually a good "mulch" and offers some protection. Many perennials are lost at high altitudes when there isn't much snow during the winter, but the temperatures are extremely cold.

> **High on a Mountain Tip:** Heavy snow on shrubs and trees can transform a yard into a winter wonderland, but get out there fairly quickly and shake the snow off limbs before they break. An early snowfall while leaves are still on the trees can cause damage as the added weight of the snow on the foliage can break limbs.

once the snow melts, there they are—some looking like peeled bananas with the banana missing, some resembling an upside-down, slightly squished octopus, with others showing off their best imitation of a ground cover. Keep this under control by wrapping them. (See page 40.)

Fruit trees will pretty much fend for themselves during their dormant season if you gave them a deep watering back in November. Remembering to paint or wrap young trunks would help as well. (See page 41.)

> **High on a Mountain Tip:** Take care when using salt to keep driveways and sidewalks free of ice. This same salt can get into the lawn and flowerbeds and cause salt damage.

PERENNIALS

Perennial flowers—those which you are hoping against hope will come back next year—need little care during the deep winter months. Newly-planted perennials would benefit from a layer of mulch after the soil is frozen.

The few perennial food crops that die to the ground in the winter have good sense to just shed their leaves and lie low until spring returns. Shhh! They're sleeping. At least, you hope they are—only spring will tell for sure. When the red domes of new rhubarb growth shuffle through the mulch, you can breathe that lovely sigh of "I knew they would!" The same goes for the pointy spears of asparagus.

FEBRUARY THAW

February sometimes gives us glimpses of spring to come—Witch Hazel is blooming. Occasionally, there is a break in the snow cover that reveals daffodils and crocuses poking little green leaves up for a check on the weather and exposes brave pansies that are still in bloom under the snow. Even tulips have been known to make an appearance. When the next expected snow or cold forecast is announced via the weather guys, there is no need to run for more mulch or blankets for the early arriving bulb leaves. They know what they are doing and will survive another three feet of snow and even super cold temperatures. Calm down. Relax. They will be just fine, leave them alone and they will come soon, wagging their flowers behind them!

WAITING FOR SPRING

Since spring often takes its sweet time arriving, a gardener must find ways of fulfilling the yearning to be outside in the garden. With plans ready and seeds in hand, the anticipation is almost like a child waiting for Christmas. And yet, when looking out the window, the only thing that meets the eye are drifts of white—snow that is. So, it's back to the catalogs and back to the books—a quiet time of still dreaming about spring.

Then there are the most desperate gardeners who are seen walking about the houseplant sections of stores or the greenhouse at a nursery, breathing in the heady smell of . . . moist soil, mixed with compost? Ah, yes, the rich fragrance of gardening that makes the wait until spring a little more bearable.

Finally, the day will come when at first a nearly

indiscernible feeling fills the air, telling us that spring is on the way. Suddenly—there it is—the first pointy flower of an awakening bulb, and the wait is over!

March, April, and May

MARCH, APRIL, AND MAY

MINI GLOSSARY

Cotyledon	A leaf of the embryo of a seed plant, which upon germination either remains in the seed or emerges, enlarges, and becomes green. Also called a seed leaf.
Small Fruits	Fruits not from trees—grapes, berries, currents, and so on.
Lug	To carry an awkward or heavy object; or a box for fruit and vegetables.
Overseed	To add grass seed to an existing sparse lawn to create a thicker healthier lawn or to fill in the spaces left after power raking.
Starts	Small, young plants.
Succession Planting	Spacing time of the planting of vegetables to ensure a continuous harvest rather than having the entire crop ready all at once.
Work the Soil	To dig deeper than one or two inches into the soil and turn the soil over—usually involves shovel, spade, digging fork, or tiller.

MUSINGS

March is such a tease. *"Ah, look! The snow is gone! Yippee!"* The next day brings nine inches of new snow. *"Oh, look! The snow is gone! Hooray!"* The next day brings a torrential downpour of sleet and rain. *"Oh goodie, the snow is gone! Tomorrow the ground will be ready to plant peas!"* The next day brings the hardest frost in recent memory followed by seven inches of new snow.

You have to love a month that *giveth* and *taketh*

away with such innocent zeal. Going from sweaters to snow boots in twenty-four little hours will really keep gardeners on their toes. But this type of weather is truly the harbinger of the long-awaited spring. From kites to clippers, we have our tools at the ready, and here we go!

Spring Lawn

LAWNS

The neighbor with the greenest lawn this time of year was probably the one out spreading a winterizing fertilizer just barely before the snowstorm in October. Or maybe just *after* the first snowstorm in October.

FERTILIZING

It isn't the fertilizer in the spring that makes the difference between a tannish, straw-looking front lawn and a lovely spring-green patch of grass.

Of course, if that little chore fell right off your to-do list last fall, you can apply a light fertilizer in March or April. Since it will be best for the lawn if you don't actually use a sprinkler to water it until around May 1st-ish, pay attention to the local weather folks and get out there a day or so before a predicted rain/snowstorm. Then *you'll* be that crazy gardener with rain hat on head and fertilizer spreader in hand, whirring like crazy to beat the storm.

Stay away from the "weed and feed" type products. Getting the "weed" part to actually hit the leaves of the weeds and stay there is iffy at best. Much more effective is the attack-one-weed-at-a-time approach. At least, that way you are less likely to be exposing every blade of grass, every passing kitty, and every child's foot to chemical poison.

OVERFERTILIZING

Over fertilizing goes right along with overwatering as a major source of ground water pollution; plus the succulent growth of grass forced to grow quickly is much more susceptible to any passing lawn disease. It's tastier to the insect hordes as well—overfertilizing is nearly an "Eat at This Lawn" sign for passing bugs. One fertilizer application in the fall can be sufficient. Lawn growing in loose sandy soil may benefit from another application toward the end of April.

RAKING

Those raking muscles are already tensing for another go. This *should* be an easier time because you *did* rake everything up one last time in the fall, right? Well, the sooner you can get all those leaves off of the grass the better.

NEW LAWN

Weather and soil permitting, springtime is the second best time to put in a new lawn. (The first and best time, remember, is fall.) Late May is really pushing the limit, though, at least for using seed. Baby grass plants suffer from high temperatures, direct sun, and drying winds. Sod can be put down anytime, if you prepare the soil properly and have the ability to water well every day for a week or so. (See pages 15–21 for how to plant a lawn.)

CORE AERATION

Much like putting in a new lawn, core aeration can be done either in the spring or the fall. It ought to be done one time or the other. (See page 21 for explanation of core aeration.)

OVERSEEDING

Power raking may be useful if you want to thicken up an older or sparse lawn. It will cut through weeds as well as grass plants, leaving the soil between what is left ready to overseed. You can also simply rake the lawn vigorously by hand and get the same results.

Rake the entire lawn, removing all the dead or loose plant material. If there seems to be a lot of bald dirt spots when you are done, don't worry. If the lawn seems to have just a little too much space between blades of grass, that's okay too. The over-seeding process is meant to fill in the spaces, small or bald, with new baby grass plants. The soil will be kind of ruffled up when you did the raking, by hand or power machine.

If some areas still seem a little packed down and flat, do a little more raking to create very small ridges and furrows. Thoroughly water the area a day or so before you start to overseed to allow the water to soak down at least 5 or 6 inches. Lightly go over the area with a hand rake one more time. Grass seed must make contact with the soil to germinate and these little bumps add more places to the soil surface for that contact to be made.

Apply the seed at half the rate listed on the package. If the directions say 1 pound of grass seed will cover 1000 square feet, only spread ½ pound per 1000 square feet. The seed will be more evenly distributed if you use a WhirlyBird or drop spreader. Put down half of the seed while walking east and west, the other half while walking north and south. If you find yourself slightly directionally challenged, spread half the seed walking toward and away from the house and the other half walking back and forth in front or behind the house.

The seeds need to be in firm contact with the soil. Walking on the bare spots or tamping them down with the back of a garden rake should take care of that. Any remaining lawn, be it ever so humble or sparse, will help hold the moisture needed to keep the little seeds damp until they germinate. But if in the coming days the temperatures go sky-high, you will probably need to sprinkle the whole area up to three or four or more times a day

Because there are baby grass plants out in the mature lawn you will need to stop mowing until the little blades are at least an inch and half long. Don't you hate it when you can't mow every week? (For some of you, that may not be so bad.)

MOWING

Mowing and edging begin in Earnest—or Kearns or Pittsburgh or wherever you may live—during May and possibly even April. Bluegrass or fescue lawns should be kept 2½ to 3 inches long. Yes, that is *after* mowing. Edging is more of a satisfying exercise than a necessary step in keeping a lawn looking good—unless you live in a neighborhood where lawn keeping has been raised to a worshipful status. In that case, you better put edging on your weekly "Obligatory Duties" (OD) list.

Bluegrass has a tendency to grow in nearly every direction except the one you want it to. With the ability to invade a flower bed and hide all but the tallest roses, you'd think it could fill in that little bald spot someone caused by mistaking dandelion killer and kills-everything killer. But no, it isn't so. Left on its own, that little bald spot will quickly be covered by a half a dozen or so noxious weeds before you can even *say* bluegrass.

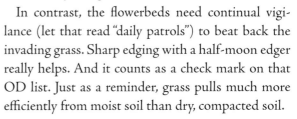

In contrast, the flowerbeds need continual vigilance (let that read "daily patrols") to beat back the invading grass. Sharp edging with a half-moon edger really helps. And it counts as a check mark on that OD list. Just as a reminder, grass pulls much more efficiently from moist soil than dry, compacted soil.

Fescue on the other hand is a "clump" grass. The growing pattern is one of peaceful co-existence rather than invading like little green hordes. Just as it suggests, clump grass slowly grows by enlarging the clump. Sounds good? (Except if a patrol path is worn across a corner of the lawn by the resident Pekinese! No way will that fill back in during your lifetime.) Overseeding is usually an annual job with a fescue lawn that has bald spots or bald swaths. But if you have an area that gets little wear and it is next to flower or vegetable beds, you'll learn to love fescue's "grow and let grow" attitude.

TREES IN LAWN

Trees—because you put them there on purpose or someone before you did—are sometimes found growing in the lawn areas of a landscape. Both lawn and trees have their places, but they were never meant to live together. The needs of grass and trees are vastly different. Watering frequency, fertilizer, and even the necessary organisms in the soil are different for each. Try to place the trees in a "tree only bed" or at least a shrub or flower bed area. Should trees somehow have found their way into your lawn, at least keep the grass back from the trunk of a minimum of 18 inches. That means an area *at least* 3 feet across around every tree. And no flowers ought to be planted there either, so get that vision of petunias or marigolds right out of your mind. What *does* go there? Organic mulch or gravel could be applied. And if it is over a weed barrier that will help halt the grass or weed invasion, so much the better.

WATERING

Both cool season grass types—bluegrass and fescue—will always look their best in the spring and fall. If asked their preference for a summer activity,

they would always vote for turning tan and going dormant—a plant's equivalent of hibernation. But that is seldom allowed to be the answer to the question, *"And what are we going to do this summer?"* The answer instead is, *"Grow, grow, grow! Green, green, green!"*

To keep the little grass plants from going into a fatal funk, gardeners should remember to mow long, water deeply but infrequently, and hold off on the fertilizer until fall. If the lawn requires 1½ inches of water per week, it would be better to put down more of the water less often instead of a little every day. When you use this spring as a training time for deep root growth and mow at the recommended height, there should be NO reason to water every day, even in sandy soil. Folks who get irrigation water turns every 7 to 10 days grow wonderfully green thick lawn, so there . . . go and do likewise!

Granted, lawn that hasn't been encouraged to grow deep roots or has been mown way, way too short will look right miserable during the hot summer months, but right now it should still be happy with less water than most folks apply. In the Intermountain area, it is recommended that you don't water at all until after the first of May, or even a couple of weeks later than that if spring has been fairly wet. Lawn roots grow down to find the moist soil, so letting the top dry out during the March, April, May period will encourage that deeper growth. Moisture from winter is still just below the surface, so as long as the top of the soil is

dry, the plants will seek the deeper water level.

This training of deep root growth is essential if you want your lawn to look as good in July as it does during the spring months.

Spring Fever

CALL OF THE OPEN SOIL

Ah, the call of the open soil! The urge to plant is irresistible. But hold on there, anxious gardener, while I tell you the Tale of the Adobe Clods.

It was a fair morning decades ago when I surveyed my little Kingdom of Gardening. Back in my boundless energy of youth, nearly every square foot of our backyard was set to produce a bountiful harvest. Two peach trees—Early Elberta and Lemon Elberta— were in beautiful pink glory. Both the blackberry and the boysenberry bushes were beginning to throw out their soon-to-be 15-foot-long canes. The strip of asparagus patch was still hiding its treasure, but the green spears would soon be poking out of the ground. Strawberries, shedding their winter brown coats of old leaves, also promised treats to come. Ah, yes, all was right in the garden.

Then the itch began. It started as just a little tingle at the ends of my thumbs, it soon spread to every finger. Early peas, I thought. *This* year, I'll have early peas. I didn't get my garden duties completed the previous fall, but, hey, I dug in tons of compost earlier that season, didn't I? That soil should be just perfect for a row of early peas. So my tingling fingers plus thumbs took up my trusty shovel, and I began to turn over the soil. Well, look at that! The soil didn't crumble when it fell from the end of the shovel; it just sort of plopped. So for the length of the garden I plopped my way through an entire row. What a lumpy mess! But my tingling digits were not to be denied. Ah ha! I'll just smooth out a narrow area with the rake and that should work. Oh, it worked for the row

High on a Mountain Tip: Don't be fooled by a period of warm weather in the early spring which makes you want to rush out and start planting. There will be another frost! Plant early to have a longer growing season, just make plans for protection from the cold.

Be prepared with coverings for your garden so that when an unexpected cold night threatens, the plants can be covered and protected. There are commercial frost blankets to use, or old blankets and sleeping bags work as well. A few degrees will make all the difference.

of peas, all right. And I am happy to report we *did* have early peas.

We also had large cantaloupe-sized clumps of soil that dried to the brick consistency of adobe. Adobe, as I later learned, is simply soil, organic matter (usually straw, but turns out compost is a fine little substitute), water, and enough plopping to beat most of the air out of the resulting clump. Hmmmmm. Okay, I thought, I'll just pound on them with the back of the shovel like I usually do with little clumps of soil. Whoa! Even with a hammer, I couldn't get much more than a chip off of those clods. That summer, my vegetable patch had a border of adobe clods. "How clever," visitors would say. "What a novel idea!" Yeah, right. It wasn't until the next spring after nature did its very thorough job of freezing and thawing through the winter that I got my soil back from the clutches of the Adobe Clods.

So beware, my gardening friends, of the fidgeting fingers, the thrumming thumbs, and the allure of the early peas. Don't get suckered into working soil that is still too wet!

WORKABLE SOIL

The test for workability of the soil is easy—dig down about 4 inches and scoop up a handful of soil. You may need a trowel for this first step. Now squeeze the soil in the palm of your hand. Does water squish out between your fingers? When you open your hand does the ball of soil still show the imprints of your fingers? Then, my friend, it is *too wet*.

However, if the soil feels a little like a dark chocolate cake, crumbly and soft, and the ball breaks apart easily when you bounce the soil in your hand or drop it to the ground, you are in business, good gardener, so go claim your chance at early peas!

If you have light and sandy soil, you will be able to plant earlier than the gardener with heavy, clay soil. Sandy soil simply warms up and dries out faster than clay soil.

If you choose to do your vegetable gardening in a raised bed full of good, loamy, organically-enriched soil, you'll be just that much further ahead each spring. Soil in raised beds dries out faster and doesn't need roto-tilling so it is ready to plant earlier in the spring than those folks with existing sandy or clay soil. (See page 23 to see how to create a raised bed.)

> **Extra Bonus Box:** Christmas lights placed under plastic or a bed sheet cover will give plants a few extra degrees of warmth when needed.

Early planting—when the soil is ready—is a therapeutic exercise. *Early* is a relative term however. If you prepared the soil the preceding fall, use raised beds, have loose sandy soil, and are nestled in at least Zone 5 or warmer part of the country, early planting may be as soon as the middle of March. Gardeners enjoying none of the above may be lucky if they can start planting by the middle of May.

> **Bonus Box:** Choose and select varieties of plants that grow and mature in a shorter period of time. Read the seed packets and don't plant crops that take 120 days from planting to maturity if you only have an average of 90 frost-free days in your growing season.
>
> "Days to maturity" on a seed packet may mean days from transplanting or days with good growing conditions.

Vegetables

PLANTING SPRING VEGETABLES

When you set out to plant vegetable seeds in the spring, the soil may be still moist from the winter snow or rain. In that case, just plant as recommended and then sprinkle water lightly to settle

> **High on a Mountain Tip:** Making and using a cold frame to protect and acclimatize plants in a cold climate helps get the season off to an earlier start. A cold frame is a bottomless box topped with usually an old window tilted to the south to catch the suns rays. It should be airtight but easily vented. Lift and prop up the window to provide air circulation, but be sure and lower it early enough to trap the warm air before night. A hot bed can be made by adding an electric gardening heating coil to warm it up further.

the soil around the seeds.

If the soil has dried out in the top 3 or 4 inches, water the day before you intend to plant or several days before if you have clay soil. You will still water lightly after planting in this case as well.

If you decide to start plants from seeds and they successfully sprout up and are ready to go outside, remember to harden them off before planting in the garden. This is done by setting the seedlings outside for a few hours in a sheltered location, leaving them out a little longer each day until they can stay out all day and all night. A week or two of doing this should acclimate your plants so they'll grow and flourish when transplanted.

Bonus Box: Fancy glass garden cloches ("bell" in French) have been used since the 1800's to protect single plants from the weather. Today, something similar can be done using pop bottles or milk jugs with the bottom removed and placed over a plant with 1 inch of the container going down into the soil. The cap can be taken off during the day for ventilation and replaced at night to help hold in warmer air. Make a hole in the handle of a milk jug and push a stake down through to hold it in place during wind.

Make mini-greenhouses of any desired size over your plants using thin PVC pipe bent in hoop shapes and slipped over pieces of rebar that have been pounded halfway into the ground. Cover the structure with plastic and secure. Be sure and vent the plastic when the sun in shining or the plants will cook inside. This can be made as large or small as you would like. This can also protect newly planted seeds from washing away during heavy rainstorms.

High on a Mountain Tip: Lay down either black or clear plastic over a garden area to melt the snow quicker. This can also be used to warm up the soil before planting.

If you can't get your garden covered up and a frost is predicted, turn on the sprinkler at night when the temperatures drop. Surprisingly as water turns to ice, it gives off heat and keeps plants warmer than the air around them. Keep the sprinkler going until the temperature warms up and the ice melts.

Early crops enjoy, or at least tolerate, both cool soil and cool air. Some veggies even demand coolness or they will produce little and what you harvest is likely to be hard, bitter, dry, or all of the above.

In the early cool category are peas, lettuce, broccoli, spinach, radishes, and cauliflower. Other veggies that are a little more flexible but can still be planted fairly early include beets, carrots, chard, onions, and potatoes. By mid April, all of the vegetables listed above grow well in the garden and are safe to plant without much worry about frost damage. For our Zone 3 and 4 gardening friends—check out the High on A Mountain Tips.

Since you waited until the soil was dry enough to work (you did, didn't you?) before planting, adding and digging in more organic matter is always a good idea. Another two inches in the planting area makes for better soil and happier plants.

Radishes

Radishes are the sprint runners of the vegetable world. Up and growing just four to six days after planting, they should be ready to harvest in less than a month. Radishes go in cool soil in the spring, come up in a week, and should be harvested three to four weeks later for best taste.

And before you plant three rows of these speedsters, ask yourself how many radishes your family *really* eats in a week. If left in the ground too long, these whiz growers take on another trait—mouth-blistering heat. Okay, not blistering heat, but wow, can they get hot enough to make eyes water just before being spit out. Add to this the pithy middle large radishes get, and it isn't a pretty picture. So don't try to force down forty radishes because they grew to the perfect size all at once.

If you really like radishes (and it never fails to amaze me how many people do) try using *succession planting*. That is, plant about a five-foot row and then wait seven to ten days and plant another five-foot row and then ten days later plant the last row. Harvesting and eating come out almost even that way.

Bonus Box: Use a plastic knife as a plant marker, write the name of the crop and date planted in permanent marker and stick it in the row or square. While the utensils are out, use plastic forks in the garden pushed half-way in the ground with the tines up as a deterrent for kitties who think your garden is a litter box.

Radishes are a good crop for kids to watch grow. And a variety called Easter Egg adds a color surprise with each radish pulled. Some will be pink, some lavender, white, or even red. However, if your child doesn't *like* radishes, you should probably suggest they clean them thoroughly, put them in a little basket, and give a "gift from the garden" to a neighbor or the local food bank.

There isn't much that discourages a "budding" gardener like biting into the first successful harvest and finding out radishes are nasty; although, this does offer the opportunity for a lesson in diversity and different tastes. ("*Yes, sweetie, some people* do *like radishes, they really do.*")

Carrots

When you plant carrots for the first time the results may be less than stellar. It often goes something like this:

- Rake the garden smooth.
- Pound a stake into the ground at both ends of where each row will be.
- Stretch a string between the stakes to mark a nice straight row.
- Make a little furrow with your finger or the end of your rake just under the string.
- Check the package to see how many

seeds should go in this row.

- Decide they're too hard to count and just sprinkle the entire package fairly evenly in the furrow.

- Cover the little seeds, tamp down the soil, and water well.

- Tape the empty seed packet to one of the stakes to remember that the carrots are *here*.

You look out three days later and realize the paper packet isn't waterproof and is now a soggy little tatter at the foot of one of the stakes. So, you try the following scenario:

- Take a waterproof marker and write "CARROTS" on one of the stakes.

- Watch as a week later the dog chases the neighbor's cat across the garden catching the string on his collar as he goes.

- Content yourself with the fact that ONE of the stakes at the end of the row seems to be in place.

- Another week goes by, and your children and their friends are squealing with delight to find that each remaining stake makes a perfect pirate sword.

- Wonder how much carrots are selling for at the market this year.

- Because the lettuce and radishes came up in four to seven days, there are two lovely green leafy ribbons stretching across your garden.

- The onion seeds, taking at least two weeks, along with the potential carrots have simply vanished into the area now dubbed "Pirates Cove."

- Wonder again how much carrots are selling for at the market this year.

Most of that scenario will need to be dealt with on a case-by-case, dog-by-dog basis, but there is a nifty solution to the slowpoke carrot seeds.

Plant the carrots and the radishes *in the same place, right in the same row!* Radishes are up in a relative flash, marking the row for all to see. The growing radishes keep the soil nice and loose and that helps the carrot seeds break through the surface of the soil. For primo radishes, they need a lot of watering and should be picked when they are about four weeks old.

How about that! At three weeks the carrots are up between the radishes; a week later, picking the radishes thins the carrots and *everybody's* happy!

All those early season veggies are well and good. Real gardeners know it is the plants that come later that make for bragging rights. Few offices or social gatherings are the place for tales of the earliest beet or awe-inspiring stories of the largest bunch of chard. But start talking tomatoes, peppers, or melons, and heads turn!

Onions

Onion seeds are funny angular black seeds that are very, very hardy. They will grow in nearly any soil as long as the watering is fairly even. That said, a loose loam will result in larger onions. Seeds can be broadcast (scattered) in a bed, planted in a square arrangement, or placed in a long row or furrow. The emerging onion plants look like skinny, bent in half blades of grass.

Green onions (scallions) only need an inch or so between little plants. If you planted seed for larger bulb onions, thin them to 2 inches apart and pull every other one for early harvest and let the remaining ones go through to late fall for the big fat bulb onions. There are a half dozen or more varieties but the planting process from seed into the garden is the same for all.

Most garden centers sell onion sets in the spring. These are little onions that were allowed to grow to about one-half inch in diameter and then put into storage to halt their growth. The little sets look like the regular onions you buy in the supermarket, only teeny. They have no leaves and no roots. Most places carry three kinds in the spring—generic white onions, generic yellow onions (which store the longest), and generic red (usually purple in color) onions. The sets are quicker to show growth than seeds and are easier to handle when you're planting. Plant the little bulb about an inch deep and 2 to 4 inches apart.

Another way to plant onions is by baby plants. Nurseries will either start the seed early so you can buy plastic containers of onions or bring in bundles of bare root onions. Either way, the onion plants should be separated into the separate plants so they can be planted individually. Space the onion plants

the same as with the other growing methods, but the holes need to be deeper to accommodate the roots.

Consistent watering and a 2–4 inch layer of mulch will result in juicy tender onions for a salad, a sandwich, or storage.

Peas

It's hard to believe that the hard, often wrinkled, little pea will grow to a rather large vine producing dozens of sweet green pea pods. To get this miracle off to a good start, it helps to soak the seeds in tepid water for 4–12 hours. They can actually drown, so don't go off and forget them for a couple of days.

Peas can be planted as a single row in the garden but they are easier to tend in a broad planting. I create a trough about an inch deep, 4 inches across and as long as the particular bed the peas will be growing in. Scatter the now plump peas along the trough so they end up about 2 inches apart. Using the soil you took from the trough, cover the seeds about an inch deep and tamp them down—the back of a hoe, or rake, or your hand will do the job.

There are some pea varieties that need little or no support for their vines. The vast majority will need some kind of trellis or string configuration to keep the vines up and producing well. And it's easier to find the pods to pick if you aren't down on your hands and knees pushing through the pea plants.

Beets and Swiss Chard

You can tell these veggies are closely related when you see what each seed looks like. Practically identical! Each little "seed" is actually a cluster of seeds that may contain one to five potential plants. Space the seeds 1 or 2 inches apart. You'll still have seedlings growing in little groups. Thinning the beets is a necessary task if you want individual beets that are easy to harvest and have grown strongly in their own little garden space. *Don't* just pull the scrawniest two or three tiny plants—snip them off with a pair of scissors, if possible. Pulling out those nearby babies will disturb the

roots of the remaining plant. This is true for any seedlings you need to thin—although if you gently dig the entire clump and carefully tease the extra beets apart, you can often plant them in another spot in the garden.

Chard will grow just fine as a multi-plant grouping. If you haven't tasted chard, you've missed a real treat. Steamed or lightly braised this extremely vitamin-packed vegetable tops spinach hands down in my book. And chard is slow to bolt so you can enjoy it through an entire season.

Bonus Box: Rhubarb chard and bright lights chard make a colorful addition to the flower border as well as the veggie garden.

Lettuce

Lettuce can be planted by seeds or little plants called "starts" or transplants. Either way, their growth needs to occur while the air is still relatively cool. Water should be consistent, with *no* dry spells in between soakings. With cool weather and even watering, lettuce will be sweet and crisp.

Because lettuce seeds are so tiny, take care to just barely cover the seeds—the depth of the soil should only be about twice the width of the seeds. And go ahead—let's see you try to measure that! Basically sprinkle soil or compost over the seeds and give them a little soft tamp.

Broccoli and Cauliflower

If you have your garden all ready to plant, these vegetable can be planted by seed as soon as the soil is dry enough. Plant the little round seeds about one-half inch deep, two seeds to a hole. Clip the smallest plant off at the ground if both seeds start to grow. These crops take a lot of space so plant the seeds a foot apart in all directions.

Potatoes

Seed potatoes aren't seeds! Nope, they are either little potatoes or pieces of larger potatoes. Nurseries and garden centers carry these seed potatoes and sometimes have as many as eight to ten different varieties. There is an excellent reason to buy these certified potatoes rather than cutting up the store bought produce. "Certified Disease Free" on the label of the 50- or 100-pound bag that comes into the nursery means there will be no *diseases of potato plants* that will affect your crop or soil. Plus the certified seed potatoes have not been treated with anything to keep them from sprouting, and your market potatoes have.

Potato plants take quite a bit of space and the yield per square foot isn't great. Oh, the flavor of homegrown potatoes makes up for all of that. And many of the varieties you can grow at home just aren't available in grocery stores. Some don't ship well, others don't store well, and still others do not grow uniformly enough for consumer's picky ideas of produce perfection.

Sandy loam is ideal for potato growing. If you have really heavy soil, make sure you amend your potato patch thoroughly. Although these plants aren't water guzzlers, they do need consistent moisture up to a week or two before harvest. If you let the water in the soil go from moist to dry for a while and then back to moist, you'll most likely have funny nobbley potatoes. Each time the soil dries out, the plant figures it's done growing the tubers and sort of closes off the existing potato. Whoops, more water equals more growing, but instead of continuing where it left off, the potato kind of starts over. So now the original potatoe has a new knob of growth on its side. You can end up with some really bizarre and comical potatoes, but they are real stinkers to try and peel.

If you pick out little golf ball sized seed potatoes, you can plant them whole. With the larger ones you need to cut the potato into 4 or so pieces, each with three or four "eyes." Let the cut pieces dry for a couple of days before you plant. Potatoes are actually swollen stems, not roots, so the "eyes'" are the buds that will form the stems and roots. It is from the portion of the stems that are underground that the potatoes grow.

This is why you read of "hilling the potatoes." Plant the seed potatoes, or pieces, about 4 inches deep and 1½ to 2 feet apart. When the dark, crinkly leaves poke out of the soil, cover them with 4 inches of loose organic soil or mulch. When they poke out again, cover them again! This doesn't discourage the plant; it just makes sure there is a lot of the new stem below ground. That's what makes for plenty of potatoes.

HARVESTING COOL SEASON CROPS

Peas

Planting early allows you to harvest during the cool season. To get the sweetest peas, cauliflower, broccoli, radishes, and lettuce, harvesting needs to be done before the heat of June descends. Pick regular peas before the pods are fat and full of peas. The whole point of planting your own peas is to get to them while they are still young and tender. The edible pod, or snap peas, can have pods that are quite round in cross section and still be yummy because you eat them pod and all. Snow peas—the flat pods used for stir fry—should be picked while the pod is still, well, flat! The peas inside should be very tiny. Once the peas (of any variety) get so large that they completely fill the pods and are packed tightly, they will become dry and woody.

Not all is lost if you missed picking them at their prime. Let them continue to mature until the pod is tan and completely dried and you can harvest the seeds for next year's garden.

Broccoli and Cauliflower

It is tempting to buy little cauliflower and broccoli plants that already have tiny heads developing while the plants are still in the plastic containers at the nursery. *Do not be fooled!* That premature development will never grow into the lovely, tender broccoli or cauliflower head that you hoped for. Growth was stunted and the plant put out a last futile gasp of desperation in hopes of being able to produce flowers and seeds. Yes, flowers! Both broccoli and cauliflower produce the tight heads of flower buds that we call yummy, but if left to grow longer each bud opens to a tiny yellow flower and eventually produces seeds.

Your task as a gardener is to interrupt that process right at the moment the buds are rounded and tightly packed by cutting the head off. Be sure to take measures to remove any little hitchhikers that came to the kitchen hidden in the harvest. You probably don't want to know how many different *kinds* of critters may be tucked away in a head of broccoli or cauliflower but a soak in salty water or water with a couple of tablespoons of vinegar will bring them squirming to the surface. Don't look too close—just drain off the water and rinse the heads well. Now you are ready to eat raw, steamed, or boiled (last choice for good flavor) broccoli and cauliflower. Add a little lemon juice to the cooked ones and savor the flavor!

Onions

By pulling every other onion in a row or block, you will leave space for the others to get larger through the season. Regular bulb or globe onions can be harvested early when they look like scallions, but if left in the ground they will enlarge to the round or oblong shapes by the end of the season. Real scallions, green onions, will stay long and narrow for the entire growing season.

Lettuce

There are two equally fine ways to harvest leaf, or loose leaf, lettuce: start cutting the outside leaves, two or three per plant, as soon as eight or so leaves have developed. By cutting the outside leaves the plant puts more energy into growing new, inner leaves. This allows for the very earliest fresh greens for your spring salads. Add a couple of sliced young radishes, a scallion or two, and winter is officially banished from your dining table.

The other method of harvesting both leafy and head varieties of lettuce is to let them reach maturity and pull up or cut the entire plant to the ground. This provides larger quantities of the greens all at one time for whatever lovely use you put them to in your kitchen. Of course, this also eliminates any further harvest as the plant will not grow back.

TENDER OR WARM-SEASON CROPS

After the last average frost date. (See Frost Chart on **page 141**.) these tender crops *can* be planted but most years the "average" will do little to determine the arrival of descending frosts. For most areas it is still better to wait a couple of weeks past that date to set out little transplants without added protection. If you are planting summer squash, cucumbers, or even tomatoes by seeds in the garden, those extra two weeks are especially important.

Soil temperature is important to good plant growth. We usually try to avoid freezing the noses off little veggie plants but forget to avoid chilling their toes as well. Soil can be warmed by covering the area to be planted with clear (adds 4–6 degrees) or black (warms 2–4 degrees) plastic over the planting area a couple of weeks before planting. Remember to secure all of the edges of the plastic with boards, rocks or soil to avoid seeing your warming blanket fly by the window during a fierce windstorm. Before you set a little plant in its hole, fill the hole with very hot water, and let it drain completely. This gives a little extra warm boost to the newly planted roots.

After all your little veggies are snug in their garden beds, you still need to be cautious about leaving them on their own out in the harsh garden world. A random late frost can kill them on the spot. Covers for a night or two (or three or four or five) can make the difference between getting off to a good growing start vs. starting over again with new plants. It usually takes putting *something* between the plant and the cold air to save the day—or actually the night. A little hat, like young pirates wear, made of newspaper can be sufficient unless there is some wind preceding the cold air. Then the hat will join the plastic flying by your window. A box with a rock on top (to hold it down) or even an actual blanket will do the trick. Cold air sinks so *anything* over the plants will help. If the plants are small enough, a gallon milk jug with the bottom removed can do a very good job of protection.

Old time farmers used to test the warmth of the soil by dropping their drawers and sitting for a few minutes. Couldn't take it for more than a few seconds? Good indication the soil is still too cold. Now, mind you, the closest next-door neighbor was probably a mile away and it was at least five miles to the nearest road. This is not the recommended procedure today. If you choose to test the theory, we disavow any knowledge of where you might have gotten that silly idea.

The average last frost date is a good, modest measure of whether it is time to plant the tender crops. Generally, it is safe about two weeks after the usual last frost date. Check your local Agricultural Extension Office for that information. In the Intermountain area, Zones 5 and 6 can aim for the middle of May.

Tomatoes, peppers, and melons are part of the "tender" or warm season crops. Others in this group include summer squash, cucumbers, pumpkins, corn, beans, and eggplant. Warm season plants really do demand warm weather. It means the *air* and the *soil* should be warm. The air should be 50 degrees and above both day and night, and the soil at least 60 degrees. Corn and beans are usually grown from seed, but those seeds will just sit and sulk in cool soil.

PLANTING EARLY

There are a few intrepid, undaunted, gardeners who just won't wait that long. That's why Walls O' Water and black plastic mulch were invented. Well, that's why the Walls were invented anyway. If you choose to defy the odds and put your plants in harm's way, just remember, you need to warm the soil as well as protect the plants from the frosty air. Cold feet may not have the dramatic effect that a blast of unexpected

snow does—all those black, curled leaves and all—but the shock can set the little plants back so far they may never recover. It's your call when to plant. And it's good to remember most local nurseries grow extra plants just for that reason. They are pleased to sell you tomato plants again, and sometimes yet again, and in late snow years, even another time after that!

PLANTING BY SEED

Most warm season vegetables have a fairly long growing season—70 to 110 days of frost-free growing. There are some cucumbers and summer squash that mature quickly enough to plant from seed. In fact, they often mature beautifully even if the seeds are planted in July! (That is, in Zone 5.) Most of these tender crops are usually grown from transplants because the growers have greenhouses to protect the young plants and that gives them a 14 to 21 day head start over seeds you might plant in the ground. Remember these plants will not live through frosty nights unprotected and really hate to put their roots into even cool soil.

Tomatoes

Tomatoes planted before June in Zone 5 require the gardener to be on the alert for late spring cold snaps. If you want to go ahead and take a chance, see **page 114** for planting tips. And, if the tomato plant is quite large, go ahead and use the trench method described there.

Melons

Ruffling or disturbing roots will set melons and cucumbers back in their growth and may even cause them to go into a blue funk and not grow at all. Early planting without many extra precautions just won't

High on a Mountain Tip: Use commercial water walls to surround tender plants in the early spring. The water heats up during the day and keeps the plants warmer throughout the cool nights. Good to use on tomatoes, peppers, squash—anything you would like to have an early start or which has a longer growing season.

put you much ahead in the melon patch. Be sure to warm the soil with a plastic mulch and see the planting instructions on **page 109** if you just can't wait until June.

In Addition to Veggies

When you approach the adventure of planning and planting your first vegetable garden, it's easy to get fixated on just the veggies. We recommend you consider an integration program to introduce your lovely tomatoes to basil and a few marigolds and nasturtiums. Flowers play well with others, even their practically-minded vegetable and herb cousins.

The mix of plants accomplishes some very helpful jobs in the garden. The flowers attract pollinating insects to boost the production of many plants. Several herbs, like dill and fennel, also attract predatory insects. Those are the good guys that eat the bad guys. When rows or squares of different crops are mixed up it can confuse some of the less desirable pests. A cabbage moth will flit down an entire row of young cabbages depositing eggs that grow into green Cabbage Loopers. These little green "inch worms" can devour much of your cabbage heads before you ever get them to harvest size.

But if, right next to the first cabbage, you have planted a bright yellow nasturtium, then a few radishes and beyond that basil plants, the little butterfly gets confused, gives up, and flits off to somebody else's garden where the laying of eggs is easier.

Another reason to plant flowers and herbs amongst the vegetables is the delightful crazy-quilt effect of red geraniums, purple and yellow beans, bushy pepper plants, spiky onions, and dazzling golden nasturtiums. Charming! And with purple basil for extra dark color, chives adding their lavender flowers, and a Golden Sage plant on the corner it will be positively inspiring.

GROWING HERBS

For millennia people in all parts of the world have used, and sometimes misused, herbs. These versatile plants can find themselves right at home tucked in among the vegetables or flowers. The traditional "herb garden" is certainly an option but for a start just put them where they look good! Sure, they are a multi-talented group of plants that find uses in the kitchen, first aid kit, on the cosmetic shelf, or tucked into the crafter's corner. But just like a marigold that is planted 'cause it's pretty, so too can herbs be planted just because you like the way they look.

Try a few for "pretty," and you will be hooked on finding more herbs and more uses for them. Then if you are inclined to plant in straight lines or perfect squares or symmetrical patterns, I think herbs will become some of your favorite choices of plants in your garden. If you are an aspiring chef or a cook that loves depth of flavor in your food creations, you'll love walking in the garden to clip and snip some *really* fresh herbs for your dish, whether it's a soup, salad, quiche, main course, or bread. Is there a difference between dried herbs and fresh? You bet your dill there is! And, you ask, are there any advantages over the little plastic packages in the grocery store? Sure! Ten steps to the garden needing zero gasoline to get there, no extra packaging, free (okay, maybe not quite) for the picking, and you know exactly what was sprayed on the leaves and worked into the soil.

The fragrance keeps me growing herbs even if I use them for no other purpose. Imagine brushing by and releasing a heavenly aroma. I love growing an annual

herb called Sweet Annie. It is a feathery plant that grows up a single stem and by fall can be 5–7 feet tall. As I walk by, I take the stem in my hand and just lightly run my fist up the stem—oh, how sweet it is! Since I just let it go to seed every year, the next year I am pleasantly surprised to see where it decided to pop up. Being easy to pull, it just doesn't qualify as a weed in my garden. If it ends up too close to the tomatoes, out it goes, imparting a light fragrance to my gloves as I toss it into the compost bin.

How about something with a lemon scent? Well, I'm a sucker for anything lemon-scented. There is lemon balm, lemon thyme, lemon verbena, lemon basil, lemon grass, and creeping lemon thyme growing in my garden—just scattered about really, with no pattern or confinement. I hope to add lemon-scented geranium soon if I can find it.

Herbs may be annuals, biennials, or perennials, and most herbs I grow are tough perennials. However, the garden wouldn't be complete without lemon basil and lemon verbena—both very tender annuals. Remember, just because a tag *says* perennial it doesn't necessarily mean it will be in *your* area. Many a rosemary plant has gone on to plant heaven because somebody growing in Zone 4 or 5 or even 6 believed every word on the little rosemary's tag.

There are some herbs that are tough as weeds but delightful as all get-out. Give a few of them a try and don't worry about where to plant them—they go anywhere you want them to, in any part of your garden.

Chives

Chives are tasty little grass-looking plants that have an extra bonus of pretty lavender flowers every spring. Unlike grass, however, these leaves are hollow like thin, green straws. Baked potatoes are often sprinkled with finely chopped chives, so you have probably seen them even if you wouldn't recognize the plant. The leaves grow to a foot or so tall, and the thin flower stalks stand above that. Once cut, the leaves grow back giving you year-round fresh chives.

Chives are a member of the onion family, and the taste and smell let you know that right away. Individual plants grow in a clump that gets larger over many years. Any time you or someone else would like more of your chive plants just dig the clump, separate out a few or many of the plants and there you go! Each plant looks like a tiny green onion and can be grown separately, but they look better if a bunch are kept together when transplanting. Not only can you chop the leaves all season long, but in the spring you can also eat the little individual flowers. They too taste like an onion, but they carry a tiny little kick of heat as well. Just don't eat the flower *stalk*—it's woody and tough.

There are two ways to get more chives in your garden—divide an existing plant, or let the flowers go to seed. And when they go to seed, they really go to town—and just about everywhere else, too! Each small, individual flower that makes up the ball-shaped flower head will form one black seed. And *every* black seed that falls will grow. Once again, that doesn't make them weeds because they are easy to pull. But just because they are easy to pull doesn't mean it isn't very time consuming when you *need* to pull 300 chive plants.

Chives will grow in nearly any kind of soil, need no extra fertilizer, require minimal water, and thrive in direct sun down to all but the most dense shade.

Thyme

Thyme is a ground cover that doubles as a cooking herb. And thyme can be found in an upright form that grows 8–12 inches tall. One of the endearing features of this herb is the delightful flower that nearly covers the plant late every spring. The colors range from white to brilliant pink. Individually the flowers are miniscule, but blooming together they make a cloud of delightful color. Equally small are the leaves on thyme plants. Some varieties have teensy silver or golden edges around the leaves giving a sparkly effect. Most varieties of thyme can be used in the kitchen, with the exception of wooley thyme. This fuzzy, tiny-leafed ground cover is for landscape use only.

Winters don't phase a thyme plant, and they are evergreen as well as tough. I have brushed snow from my Lemon Thyme to use in the kitchen many times. The flavor is milder because there is less of the volatile oil during the cold season. The sprig of thyme still works well when bundled with two other perennials—sage and oregano—and dropped into a soup during the last ten minutes of cooking.

Thyme is purchased as little plants from a local nursery or garden center. You can usually find several different varieties of creeping thyme and maybe two or three of the upright type. Plant it in the

spring, summer, or fall, and it will do well. Sunshine requirements can be full sun down to partial shade. The upright thyme plant does get woody as it gets older and can be kept looking tidier with a vigorous trim just after flowering.

Sage

Sage isn't to be confused with the sagebrush of the west—this is a different plant family entirely. The plant may be new to many people, but the aroma is probably evocative of Thanksgiving at Grandma's house. This is the sage of turkey dress-ing fame. It can

Bonus Box: Bumblebees seem to crave sage nectar. On warm days it can look like every flower stalk has its own busy bumblebee hard at work.

grow quite large, and there are only so many calls for turkey dressing. Luckily a few of the varieties of sage shine as great additions to the general land-scape. Golden Sage has leaves with a golden green edge. Purple sage has a faint lavender tinge on the top surface of the leaves but a very purple color on the reverse side. Tri-color sage has leaves edged in cream, then pink on sage green centers. The crown-ing glory of color comes when sage blooms. Spikes of blue purple flowers cover the entire plant in mid summer.

Sage plants get very, very woody with gangly shaggy-barked stems showing in the middle of the plant and leaves only on the tip of the branches.

There is a simple method of keeping the plant look-ing fresh and full. After the third year, cut it to four inches tall every fall or you can let it grow to a rather impressive plant if you prefer. The Golden and Tri-color sage varieties grow slower and stay tidy look-ing longer than the regular variety. As a broadleaf evergreen, a sage plant gives excellent form and color to the late fall garden. And because they are on the plant all year, leaves can be dug out from under the snow when Grandma needs sage for her dressing!

Oregano

Oregano is a low-growing plant that grows rapidly to cover at least a three by three foot area. As a ground cover, it is very attractive and can be found in a golden variety which actually gives the appearance of a very bright light green carpet covering the ground. Oregano is a more aggressive herb and needs to be cared for with a firm hand. Because it roots where-ever a stem stays in contact with the soil for any length of time, you need to be lifting the stems on a regular basis. Unlike its cousin mint, oregano moves out from one central plant and the rooted stems are quite easy to pull. The flowers resemble short Hops flowers. In fact, an orna-mental variety of oregano is called Hop Flower.

There are several varieties of oregano, and the starts in the nursery are sometimes mislabeled. For a strong, biting flavor search out Greek oregano. But here's the problem: a label that reads Greek Oregano may be indeed be a generic variety. The genealogy of oregano is cloudy at best and sometimes even the growers are misled by the tags on the seeds or cuttings they receive. However, if you definitely want a more subdued flavor, Golden Oregano has a much milder taste.

Oregano is a hardy, evergreen perennial in Zone 5. But there is another plant that shares the first botanical name with Oregano and that is Marjoram; you'll see Origanum on the tags because they are both in the same genus. Marjoram is a tender plant and a true winter will kill it. Check twice to see that you have *Oregano*.

Basil

Basil is as tender as an herb plant can get. It really doesn't even like cool breezes. It can grow from 8 to 18 inches tall, depending on the variety. All can be used in cooking, even the purple-leafed types. Each variety has delicate differences in aroma and taste. My favorite is lemon basil, but I also grow sweet basil. There are basils that grow in compact little globes, ones with ruffled purple leaves and ones with exotic names like Thai or Holy Basil.

Once the soil and air warm up, basil can be planted in full sun with moderate watering. Keep cutting the top leaves and a couple of inches of stem once it grows tall enough—tall enough that you don't

remove more than half its height at once. Continual harvesting will keep the plant from setting flowers and seeds. The flavor of the leaves deteriorate once that happens.

One of the nice things about basil is that almost all full-service local nurseries carry different kinds in the spring. Just don't put the plants out too early. And if you wait until June-ish when the soil and air are warm, it grows quite easily from seed.

Dill

Often called dill weed, it most certainly is *not* a weed in my garden. Sure, it tosses its seeds willey nilley about the garden but that is part of its charm! I think it is delightful to brush up against a little ferny green plant that smells like dill pickles. Dill is an annual and likes to grow in full sun. It's not fussy about soil and only needs moderate watering.

The dill plant may grow to 3 or 4 feet in height. It is a light, airy plant that has its flowers on the top of the stems in an arrangement called an *umbel*.

This flower type lets you know that dill is related to carrots, Queen Anne's lace, and fennel among other  plants. From the tiny flowers that make up the umbel come the seeds. If you let the seeds form and fall—there you have it, dill willey nilley all over your garden!

Early morning is the best time to harvest herbs just after any dew has dried. That is when the essential oils will be their strongest. And other than dill, which is often harvested *for* its seeds, most other herbs should be cut before they have a chance to flower.

If you never harvest a single herb, it is still worthwhile to grow them. On the whole they are lovely plants that deserve a much more prominent place in the garden landscape. Besides, many are from the Mediterranean region and thrive in poor soil, hot dry summers, cold winters, and wet weather in both spring and fall. Sound like any place you know?

PERENNIAL EDIBLE PLANTS

Rhubarb

Rhubarb is a plant that should grace more gardens than it does. Some have told me they just don't *like* rhubarb pie. Now that's just silly! First of all, that pie is second only to boysenberry on the Greatest-Pies-of-All-Times list—well, *my* greatest-pies-of-all-time list, anyway. But the plant, without even being harvested for the second best pie of all time, is an impressive, almost tropical-looking addition to the  garden. When rhubarb receives enough sun and regular watering it can have leaves as big as 2 feet across! One single plant may cover an area nearly 4 feet by 4 feet and be 3 feet tall.

Grow rhubarb in a garden area with tall Canna lilies, two or three different ornamental grasses, a hibiscus or two, and you can be transported to a land far away. Make the getaway complete with a small pondless water feature, and you may never leave your backyard again.

Asparagus

Asparagus is a perennial veggie that takes space, time and serious weeding to a new high in the garden.

The upside is that an asparagus patch is forever—or nearly forever. Planting is a little involved, but after that, just keep the weeds far, far away from the asparagus, and there ya go!

Asparagus plants, or crowns, are available at local nurseries in the early spring. If you don't buy them early, you probably won't see asparagus starts again until next spring. Folks who grow asparagus usually avoid trying to grow it from seed. That is because the seeds take three years to grow enough to even *look* like asparagus plants and then another two or three years before you can start harvesting. Instead, look for "bare root" plants that resemble more than anything a very old string mop that has lost most of its strings. In the center of the mop you can barely see little teeny nubbins that sometimes have started to grow. They look like a cluster of short, little mini asparagus spears.

When you get the plants home, put them in a bucket of warm water for an hour or so while you are digging the trench. (Right, dig a *trench*, not a *hole*.) The trench should be 8 inches wide and 6–8 inches deep. Length in feet will be the number of asparagus plants times two. Once the trench is dug, there is just a little more digging that needs to be done. If you have access to well-rotted manure, the bottom of the trench would be a good place to put it. Good compost will do the job as well. The organic matter should be 2–4 inches deep, all along the bottom of the trench. Digging may be a little more strenuous here, but try to incorporate the organic matter into about six inches or so of the bottom soil. Because asparagus beds can continue producing for many years, this extra effort will really pay off with healthy plants and plenty of spears.

fern-looking kind of foliage. This is a good thing because the "fern" produces the food to be stored in order to produce the crop next spring.

CONTROLLING PESTS IN THE VEGETABLE GARDEN

As soon as vegetable plants or seeds go in the ground, a battle for truth, justice, and a bountiful harvest begins. Pests take on many forms:

- Insects, chewing and sucking types.
- Diseases, fungal, bacterial, or viral types
- Weeds, annual or perennial types
- Mollusks, slug or snail types

Weapons of choice can be:

- Hand-to-hand combat with bayonet or other sharp implement.
- Diversion to less-treasured targets.
- Biological warfare with selected diseases, poisons, and plant extracts.
- Chemical warfare with indiscriminately toxic sprays and granules.

Take the multi-legged octopus-looking plants and put them in the bottom of the trench. Straighten out the roots so they fan out more or less in a full circle around the middle—like the sunbeams you drew in first grade. Cover the row of plants with only 2–3 inches of the soil and water well. Watch for the thin little spears to come through the soil, then add two more inches of soil right over the top of them. Yep, they most likely will get buried again. Once they are up four or five inches, add the remaining soil to cover them and finish filling the trench.

Only two duties remain: put a couple of inches of mulch over the top, and don't you dare let weeds (especially grass) grow in the trench area. Then, great patience is required while you wait until the second season to harvest any spears. So, no cutting the first year, then cut only the large spears the second year for one week. From the third year on, cut and eat to your stomach's content for 4–6 weeks.

If you forget to harvest for a while, the plants may shoot right up and start forming a kind of wispy

Because Karen and I treasure life and want you and yours to live long and prosper, we will not be recommending chemical weapons in this book, although reference may be made to them. There are innumerable sources for that information elsewhere.

Hand-To-Hand Combat

The battleground will be tilted in favor of your plants if you have "grown" the best soil possible before starting your garden. That said it is still a continual war between you and the invading hordes.

Insect Control

Your plants will have the advantage if they grow at their healthy best. Eliminating stress will keep them strong and happy. (Hmmm, that works for the gardener, too!). Water needs to be applied deeply and as consistently as each crop requires. Soil should have sufficient organic matter to allow for good root growth and adequate nutrition. The bare minimum of fertilizer should be applied, and even then only if necessary.

It can be said that the very best insecticide is also the gardener's shadow. This means if you are out in the garden daily, you can spot and eliminate the invaders before they gain a foothold. A bucket of soapy water and a designated spatula or wooden spoon will be all you need to dispose of the advance scouts of many types of insects. Beetles, earwigs, and grasshoppers are among the critters that can be thwapped off of leaves and into the bucket of death. After the visible warrior has been done away, it is time to check the undersides of the leaves where it had been lurking. That is where you may find the immature reinforcements waiting to hatch. The little eggs may be white, yellow, red, green, or orange. You can take either hand-to-hand combat literally and squish them in place or be more delicate and cut off then plop the entire leaf into the bucket of death.

The underside of leaves is also the place where many of the sucking insects hide. They also love the tender new growth at the ends of twigs and shoots. Thwapping won't work with these pests. They are way too tiny for that kind of weapon. But a forceful spray from your hose will greatly reduce their numbers. (See Organic Section, page 132, for additions to your arsenal.

Slug and Snail Control

Slugs and snails are more closely related to clams than anything else that lives in your garden. The only real difference between a slug and a snail is that the snail carries its home on its back in the form of a shell. They both have rasping mouthparts and their pattern of eating often shows as long ragged holes in the middle or edges of leaves—or an altogether missing young plant.

A covert operation, under the cover of dark, will reveal many of these voracious eaters. In the light of day you may only see a silvery streak across a sidewalk or along the garden soil and plants. In the cool of the night, the eaters are revealed. I find a milk jug makes a roomy holding cell for the snails I gather from my garden. Put the lid on and dump the jug and snails into the garbage can. Do remember to put the lid on tightly. They can execute an escape and leave only an empty milk jug cell for you to find come morning.

The time-honored salt treatment really isn't too effective. Although it may give your more malicious side a little extra satisfaction to watch the writhing, foaming enemy, salt will damage concrete and a large enough amount can make your soil toxic. For those who perhaps now have their curiosity tweaked because you don't *know* that time-honored tradition,

here's how it works. Find a slug or snail. Sprinkle a little table salt on the slimy foot. Ta-da!

Slugs are a bit too slimy for me to just pick them up for disposal. Luckily, I only have their shelled cousins to contend with in my garden. (Although, I do have a friend who takes fiendish pleasure in squishing them between her heavily-gloved fingers.)

There is a product that is non-toxic to everything but mollusks. Sprinkle iron phosphate around the areas where the little creepers spend their hot, dry, days, like underneath groundcover or shrubs. You can usually find this stuff under descriptive trade names such as *Escar-Go* or *Slug-go*.

Plant Diseases

While you are on patrol, watch for the first signs of common diseases on your vegetable plants. The earliest symptoms can show up as powdery grey patches on the leaves, unusual yellow patterns, or unusual wilting of just some of the leaves on a plant.

Many diseases can be kept under control enough to enjoy a harvest without resorting to any drastic treatments. For some natural and organic methods of pest and disease control, please see page 133.

Weeds

Weeds are insidious pests. They start out so tiny, they are nearly invisible among the veggies. Then, wham, they are shading, crowding, and usurping water and nutrients to the point that the veggie plants often disappear under the onslaught. Again, the gardener's shadow is called for here. Thumb and forefinger are the tools needed to remove teeny weeds. A blowtorch and front loader come to a gardener's mind if the weeds grow unchecked for a while—and a *very little* while, at that. But keep on pulling, tugging, pulling, hoeing, digging, pulling, clipping, and pulling those

weeds. Your task, should you choose to accept it, is to prevent those weeds from flowering and setting seeds. One variation of an old saying is "One year's seeding will give you seven years of weeding." I think that is probably off by a factor of ten. It should read "*seventy* years of weeding." It is best for all concerned, friend and foe alike, if you try using an organic way to take care of weeds. (See page 132–136 for organic weed control.)

Hornets and Wasps

Sometimes the pest in the garden is after *you*, not your plants. Wasps, hornets, and bees head the list of unwanted guests at a barbeque. Sounding a wee bit like the ancients trying to appease the gods, one suggestion is to put a plate of your meal outside. Put it down ten minutes before you, family, and guests sit down for dinner. Put the plate *way*  out in the far corner of your garden. That will give the buzzing beasts time to find the goodies and be diverted from your plate.

FERTILIZING THE VEGGIES

There are some vegetable plants that are "hungrier" than others. Corn, melons, and large winter squash jump to the head of this list. First and foremost, the best way to appease their appetite is to develop a rich, organic soil. As the organic material decays, it will supply the nutrients needed for excellent growth.

For the biggest melons and squash, enrich about a 3-foot square section of soil before you plant seeds or little starts. Add 3–4 inches of good compost

and some all purpose organic fertilizer to this planting area. That is the area where the roots will need the extra nutrition the most. Local nurseries and garden centers carry a good selection of fertilizers. Just check the labels until you find "organic" and "all-purpose" on the same label!

Before planting the entire garden, it will give all your crops a boost if you add a couple of inches of compost and additional organic fertilizer. Follow all label directions for how as well as how much to apply. By the time you have added organic matter consistently for a few years and dug in as much rich compost as you can find, fertilizer needs will rarely be more than this spring season addition.

Watering Veggies

Stress from insufficient or inconsistent water will cause plants to fail to live up to your expectations. Whatever method you use to apply water, the critical issue is to keep the soil moisture constant. One of the most frequently asked questions from gardeners is, "How long and how often should I water my garden?" My fortune would have been made long ago if I could devise a formula to answer that question.

Short of making my fortune, here are some ideas to consider:

- Organic matter in the soil will allow water to get to where the plant roots need it. Add more to your garden. Okay, and then add even *extra* more.

- Water when the soil needs it. The only way to tell when to water is to check the soil—use the water meter growing at the end of your hand. (Your finger—nothing that looks like a high-tech tool!) Or you can dig down with a trowel and inspect the soil.

- Water deeply enough to soak down at least 8 inches. Check after watering to see if the water made it down that far. Your built-in moisture meter probably won't easily go through the soil that deeply so dig down with a trowel to check.

- A deep layer of organic mulch or a layer of inorganic mulch will hold the moisture in the soil by reducing loss by evaporation.

- DON'T OVERWATER. Check the soil moisture *before* you water, as well as after.

- Baby or new plants need water closer to the stem than older or established plants. It takes time for the new roots to grow out into your soil.

- Just because your squash leaves have wilted to the ground on a 100 degree day doesn't necessarily mean they need water. Drooping like a folded up umbrella is the plant's way of conserving moisture by reducing the leaf surface exposed to the hot air. Check after sundown, when the air is cooler. If they are still wilted check the soil and, if needed, give them a long soaking drink.

- Plants that have been overwatered will wilt. Wilting doesn't *necessarily* mean the plant needs water. Check the soil first.
- Plants that have been overwatered often turn light green or even yellow. Check the soil before watering again.

Water Conservation

Some areas of the country are blessed with regular gentle rains after the garden has been planted. (Or so they tell me.) My little plot of ground doesn't enjoy that good fortune. Watering—regular and thorough watering—is a necessity in my garden. Without additional water, there is simply no way I could grow vegetables, herbs, or most fruits in my arid region.

Decades ago, conservation of our water resources was thought to be a nice, if slightly quixotic, notion recommended by a few "counter-culture" types. Now it isn't just the High Mountain Desert or arid Southwest that must come to terms with finite water resources. The southeast portion of the United States balances on the edge of a water crisis. California, long an importer of water from other states, is casting about for even more sources of water for its ever-growing population. The Midwest always lives under the specter of a returning Dust Bowl event. Water conservation must now be on the high concern list of everyone.

Little seedlings and young plants need frequent watering because they have just a small amount of roots to absorb the water. As plants grow and send their roots out in all directions, sometimes even feet away from the place they are planted, watering can be less often. Whether daily or weekly, application should be slow enough to let the water penetrate down at least 6–8 inches into the soil.

The most efficient watering systems keep the water as close to the soil as possible. Sprinklers that throw water into the air before it can reach the plants lose a great deal of that water to evaporation. Gardeners can use a variety of mulches to conserve moisture once it is in the soil. (See page 45.)

It has become more convenient, cost-effective, and simple to use a drip irrigation system in the garden. Companies in the sprinkler business have come a long way with different methods to use and conserve water. Try out the many alternatives to overhead sprinklers including soaker hoses, drip emitters, and modified sprinkler heads.

Small Fruits

RASPBERRIES

Among the plants that show up bare root this time of year are raspberries. Several varieties are available, but I recommend you try only one kind at a time to begin your pursuit of the "waskily waspberry." Plant them at least 2 feet apart. (See page 27 for making a support.)

Because they grow so wantonly, it is tempting to just dig up a clump from Grandpa's or Aunt Janni's

garden. Spring is the time for moving any transplants. Be warned however, that there are sometimes plant diseases that, for whatever reason, are being kept in check in your relative's or friend's garden. Once moved to the new situation in your garden, they may unleash all of their unhealthy potential. Sharing raspberry plants has been done hundreds of times with no problem, but again you have been warned!

STRAWBERRIES

Strawberries can actually be used as an edible ground cover. When allowed to grow willey nilley, a solid mat is formed by all the baby plants produced on the runners that hit the ground and continue to grow. This takes only a year or two, and the bare soil disappears under the strawberry plants. The berries get smaller and smaller, but the only care needed for a strawberry ground cover is to mow the plants down in the fall. Raise the blade (lower the wheels) on your lawnmower and run over the entire patch. This will ensure sure the mower doesn't cut the

crowns of the plants and as an extra bonus the clippings create a cost-free mulch in the patch.

For big luscious berries, there is more care involved. Strawberry plants are usually purchased bare root in the spring. Just like it sounds, the plants have no soil around the roots. The dormant plants are usually bundled together and often look quite dead. Dormant means the green part may not have started to grow yet. "Pathetic" is an apt description for the little bundle of

strawberry plants. If you are fortunate, at least some of the plants will have broken dormancy and give you an encouraging little wave of their new green leaves. When you get the bundle home, remove the string or elastic around them and carefully tease apart the separate plants. If they seem a little on the dry side, it is helpful to soak just the stringy root part in water for 30 minutes or so.

Strawberries should be planted about a foot apart. To determine the number of plants you need for your berry patch, measure the width and length of the growing area. Multiply those two numbers together and that will give you the number of strawberry plants to buy. Since these are perennial (confidently planted to come back the next year), soil preparation needs to be thorough. Dig in an extra 2–3 inches of good organic matter. Because it is really difficult to reach in more than 2 feet to pick berries without tromping on some hiding under the leaves, the bed should be 2 feet wide if it is against a fence or wall. Four feet wide is about the maximum if you can reach from both sides. Your patch may be 10 feet wide and 25 feet long but it will be easier on you if you run a 2 foot wide path right down the middle. Two paths would be even better if you can't reach from both sides of the growing area. Because you won't be walking on the soil, the strawberry roots will grow much better. Because you won't be walking on the *strawberries*, your harvest will be much better, too!

Cane berries and strawberries need very consistent watering until they are finished producing fruit. After that, they are quite conservative in their water needs. Every week to ten days should be sufficient. Remember, this doesn't include baby first-year plants.

BLUEBERRIES

Fall was a good time to prune the cane fruit—*cane* refers to the long stems that bear raspberries, blackberries, and many other berries. But blueberries have bushes! The growing and pruning of blueberries usually takes place in areas like, oh, Washington, Oregon, upstate New York, and Minnesota. If where you live has the same conditions as one of those areas, well, you're probably already growing blueberries! For the rest of us, you are more likely to bring in enough for a blueberry pie if you fly to Oregon, Minnesota, or Maine, and bring a lug

home with you. It's easier, too. The Intermountain West has none of the conditions blueberries need to do well: humidity, acid soil, and lots of rain.

However, if you really are convinced you need to grow your own, then here are some pieces of information that may help:

- For the most part, the bushes will do better as container plants.

- Use potting soil mixed 50/50 with peat moss for the growing medium.

- Blueberries love light in the mornings but our intense afternoon sun is a little extreme, so give them a dappled or partial shade from mid afternoon on.

- Use an acidifying fertilizer, half strength, every week.

- Add a tablespoon of vinegar to each gallon of water you use to water your container.

- After the soil is frozen, put the pot on the north side of your house or other building to ensure the soil will stay frozen. The freeze and thaw cycle will certainly be death on the plant otherwise.

- Check to see if you bought a variety that needs another kind of blueberry to set fruit. Many need a pollinator or they will flower but produce no berries. Only a few varieties are self-fertile, and you'll only need one of that type to get your blueberries.

GRAPES

Individual canes of the grape vine are much like their berry counterparts—they only bear grapes, one year. The year after producing grapes those canes should be removed. In the late winter or early spring, those canes are cut back to the trunk or major cane from which they are growing. Then the new canes that haven't yet borne grapes are cut back to 15 or so buds. If you are growing the vines for the largest harvest of grapes possible, maintain 4 to 6 major canes with only 40–60 buds on the entire grape vine. Yep, that means almost all the plant ends up on the ground by the time you are done. But you said you wanted *lots* of grapes! If you are growing the vine for cover or screening this would negate the effect you are after, so be a little less *vigorous* with the pruning shears. This kinder, gentler approach to pruning will still yield an abundance of fruit— just remember the old woody parts of the vine won't bear anything. Grape

vines usually start producing by the third year in the ground, so training should begin the year after they go in the ground. That way you can train them up from a pup, and they won't turn into unmanageable dogs, tromping down and over everything around them.

PLANTING BARE ROOT STOCK

Plants in bare root form are only available to gardeners early in the spring while they are all still dormant, meaning the plants haven't put on any new growth for the year. Roses, fruit trees, vines, cane fruit, shrubs, ornamental trees, and some perennials can be found bare root. Asparagus and even rhubarb can come this way. Because the roots are out of the growing medium where they used to live, these trees and other plants are often kept in moistened sawdust, compost, or peat moss until a gardener comes along to buy them.

Since that may or may not have been enough moisture to keep the roots sufficiently hydrated, it's

always a good idea to put the plants into a bucket of water for a couple of hours before planting. If it is going to be a while (many hours or even days) before you can start planting, don't keep the roots in water and don't let them dry out either. Remoisten the packing material and wrap the roots in newspaper, burlap, or plastic

sack. Cut a few slits in the plastic since moisture will condense in there and things may start to mold.

The hole for planting a bare root shrub or tree should be as wide as the roots are when you spread them out. So, unwrap the roots and gently untangle and spread them out!

If you find any dangling dead roots, cut them off at the point where they are attached to a plump living root. Create a volcano-looking cone in the middle of the hole. This will support the plant and give some

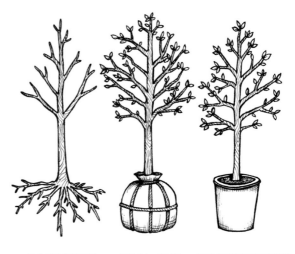

BARE ROOT   BALL AND   CONTAINERIZED
                BURLAP (B&B)

support to the bare roots. Make sure the crown is just slightly above ground level. This is usually where the plant was growing in the field before it was lifted for shipment. Soil usually leaves the bark a little darkened, and that is the sign of what should be the planting depth.

Back fill around the roots, gently settling the soil with water from a hose. The same sort of watering basin should be created as the one made when planting a container grown plant. (See page 37.)

Trees

ORNAMENTAL TREES

Spring blooming trees are glorious to behold. Masses of white, pale pink, deep pink, wine red, and pinky purple flowers greet the eye for nearly two months. Most of these beauties need little pruning. But

spring is the time to go after any errant branches. The pokey straight up suckers and water sprouts should be your target as well.

I believe the First Rule of Pruning should be: He (oh, for heaven's sake, *or she*) who has the pruners makes the rules. For it to be worthwhile (read *worthwhile* meaning *safe and productive*), there are other rules of green-thumb that should be followed:

- Never leave a stub or a stump, not even a little one. No "hat rack" pruning on your trees, no sirree.

- Always cut back to the next larger or smaller branch.

- To help the tree heal well, don't put a bandage on the cut. Good for rose bites on your arms but not for the tree. The pruning cut should be left alone with no sealant, tar, or other goop applied. If the cut was made properly, just in front of the branch collar, in a few years you won't know a branch was growing on that part of the tree.

FRUIT TREES

Fruit trees need their annual pruning about March. Apples and pears may be pruned as early as February, assuming you can slog through the snow to *get* to your trees. The others—peaches, nectarines, apricots, plums and cherries—are more likely to be "nipped" by a late spring frost. Pruning often accelerates the blossom opening and that puts the buds at more risk of being damaged by a cold snap (nipped).

Most county extension offices and many nurseries offer pruning classes every spring. Take a course or refresher course every chance you get. You only use these skills once a year, so it's reasonable to figure you've forgotten at least some of the finer points. There are many good books on pruning—the only problem is that your trees rarely look like the ones in the diagrams!

Pruning Fruit Trees

MINI GLOSSARY

Branch collar	The swollen area of trunk tissue that forms around the base of a branch.
Central leader	The main trunk of the tree.
Heading back	A branch or shoot is shortened. Older wood is headed back to an outward growing lateral. Heading back encourages lateral growth or branching.
Scaffold branch	Five to eight main (and largest) branches on a fruit tree. Should have crotches at a wide angle.
Thinning out	Entire shoots or branches are removed back to a lateral branch.

MUSINGS

The mere thought of actually taking a sharp instrument and starting to prune a tree makes many home gardeners shake in their boots. Yet, this is a not-so-difficult and even enjoyable task once the basics are understood and practiced. As you begin pruning, you'll soon get the hang of it. And, keep in mind that the tree will eventually correct any mistake you may make by growing a new branch—maybe that's comforting to you and maybe not. Pruning and making a mistake or two is much better than not pruning at all. While ornamental trees are pruned to become more aesthetically pleasing, fruit trees are pruned with the idea in mind to produce the highest-quality fruit possible. If you decide you are growing that cherry or apple tree strictly for shade and to feed the birds, just call the tree an ornamental tree and skip this pruning stuff!

The time to prune fruit trees is in the early spring while the tree is still dormant and before active, new growth has begun. Any pruning wounds will also heal more quickly during this period.

REASONS FOR PRUNING

- When fruit trees are planted with a harvest in mind, you need to take the pruners in hand to help the tree shape up and grow right. You can expect some or all of these results when proper pruning principles are applied.

- The structure of the tree becomes more open so maximum sunlight can penetrate to lower branches producing more colorful and sweeter fruit.

- The overall strength of the tree is improved.

- Limb breakage from a heavy crop or weather will be reduced.

- Fruit becomes easier to harvest.

- Any damaged wood can be removed.

- Some diseases can be prevented by allowing air circulation into the tree.

- Size and shape of the tree will be more under control

- The meddlesome branch that whacks heads of people walking by is removed.

PRUNING TOOLS

Having the right pruning tools on hand is important for carrying out the job:

- **Hand pruners:** for cuts up to ½-inch in diameter.

- **Lopping shears:** for cuts up to 1-inch in diameter.

- **Curved pruning saw:** for larger cuts.

- **Sturdy ladder** as needed.

- **Optional:** Pole pruners with a long-handle with lopping shears and a pruning saw on the end to reach high limbs without a ladder.

Don't fall to the temptation to use a regular hand saw or adjacent branches will get nicked and damaged in the process.

For branches larger than 4 inches, chain saws are preferred but should be used with extreme caution by qualified persons and with extreme caution, and always with both feet on the ground. This is another reason to prune when branches are small!

Pruning tools that are kept very sharp will make clean cuts preventing any unnecessary damage to the tree. Use a sharpening stone for hand pruners, lopping shears, and pole pruners. Pruning saws should be professionally sharpened although some have replaceable blades.

You know a scratch or cut of your skin can allow for infection from an ever-present germ. A tree is also vulnerable to infection from fungi, bacteria, or viruses when the bark is cut. To avoid making a health problem worse, tools should be kept clean and sanitized to prevent the spread of disease from infected to healthy trees. Pruning during the dormant season will also help minimize the danger of infection.

Pruning tools may be sanitized with either 70 percent denatured alcohol or with liquid household bleach diluted 1 to 9 with water. Immerse the tools in the solution for 1–2 minutes and then wipe the cutting surfaces clean. Wash tools with soap and water after use. A light coating of lubricating oil will prevent tools from rusting.

If you do suspect there is a possible disease running through your tree be doubly sure to dispose of any leaves or cut branches immediately after you finish pruning. All trimmings should go directly to the landfill—do not pass GO, do not add to your compost pile.

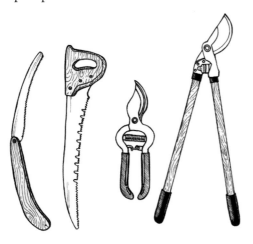

PRUNING YOUNG TREES

During the first four or five years of the life of a tree, simply prune to establish the basic framework for the tree. Just take it easy because too much pruning during this time can really slow down the development of fruit. This formative time in a young tree's life is when you need to decide which pruning method that particular tree will need and to work toward that as the tree grows. Think of this type of pruning as "training wheels" for fruit trees. This training pruning can be accomplished using just hand pruners.

If a nursery professional asks you if you'd like them to do the initial pruning on your newly purchased fruit tree, it's usually a good idea to take them up on their offer. Just like going to a doctor for the first time, I would recommend you ask a few questions first. Things like how many times have you done this before? Where did you get your training? Do *you* grow fruit trees? If you are satisfied with the answers, then it will probably be less traumatic if you turn away and admire a grape vine for a minute or two. When you turn around and see half of your peach tree on the ground *do not panic* or threaten bodily harm to the nurseryman. As you learn about the open center style of pruning, you will start to breath easier and appreciate the reduction your peach, nectarine, apricot, or sour cherry tree just experienced.

PRUNING OLDER TREES

As the tree matures, you occasionally may need to do a more thorough renewal pruning. If a tree has been pruned from the time it is young, this becomes a matter of simply following the same principles you have been following to keep the selected shape of the tree.

Perhaps you inherited, or dare we say you have neglected, a tree that has been for years without pruning. Don't try to do all the pruning at once in a single year. Plan out your approach and aim for using four to five years to achieve your goal. Consider the systems explained below and choose the one appropriate for your kind of tree. Your goal is to help the tree have a shape more closely resembling that system than, oh say, a rambling thicket. A good rule of thumb to follow is to not remove more than 20 percent of the tree's branch canopy at a time. Cutting off too many branches at once, can shock a tree and may upset the bearing of fruit for several years. Pruning an old tree using the gradual method can rejuvenate it, so you can start enjoying the "fruit" of your labor. At the very least, you will have a healthier, better shaped tree.

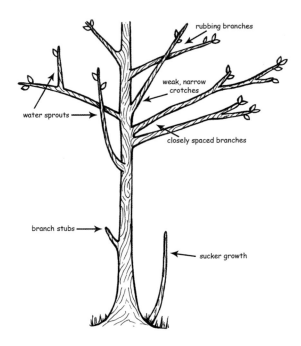

BASIC PRUNING PRINCIPLES

These basic pruning skills and techniques apply to all systems of pruning:

- Fruit trees should have five to eight scaffold branches. These should also have wide angles and will be the largest branches on the tree. Tall or long scaffold branches should be shortened.

- Remove any dead, damaged, or broken limbs that can harbor disease or pests.

While most pruning is done in the early spring, this principle can be applied anytime of the year.

- Cut out any wood that crosses or rubs on another branch or those that form narrow crotches.

- Cut off any watersprouts growing straight up from a branch in the middle of a tree or suckers shooting up around the base of the tree.

- Make all cuts next to the branch collar, which is the swollen area of bark tissue that forms around the base of a branch (See diagram A for correct pruning technique. B leaves the unwanted hatrack). As the tree heals from this cut, bark tissue will form over the cut area. If a branch collar is cut off, the tree is opened to the possibility of disease and decay because it lost its ability to heal itself, and no—you can't just put a Band-aid on it. If too much of the branch is left then the bark can't grow over the wound and seal off the cut. In other words, don't leave a stub or a hat rack on the tree!

- If a branch is large and heavy, make two cuts—one out further to remove the heavy branch and then the final cut right next to the branch collar. This way, the limb won't tear and damage the bark of the tree as the pruning cut is being made.

- If you are unsure whether to remove a branch, then don't! You can always come back later to make that decision. If you cut if off too soon, you certainly can't glue it back on! But to reduce your guilt and anguish, remember that once a cut branch hits the ground that *is* the right cut, so keep saying that to yourself and anyone who is listening.

- Pruning cuts that reduce the length of a branch should be made just above a bud.

- To keep the tree a reachable and manageable height, prune *more* branches growing up vertically and cut off *fewer* of the branches growing horizontally.

- Painting or dressing a wound from pruning is not necessary and may actually create problems with disease. Let nature do the trick!

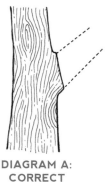
DIAGRAM A:
CORRECT

DIAGRAM B:
INCORRECT

VARIOUS PRUNING SYSTEMS

Different types of fruit trees require different pruning systems for optimal fruit production. For example, peach trees need a different pruning system than apple trees.

Apple, pear, and sweet cherry trees can be trained and pruned using either a central-leader or modified-leader system. European plums do best under the modified-leader system.

CENTRAL-LEADER SYSTEM

A central leader is the main trunk or stem of the tree from which other lateral branches develop and grow. Pruning for this method is done by thinning out the lateral branches.

MODIFIED-LEADER SYSTEM

In this more preferred system, the central leader and three or four lateral branches are given equal prominence by keeping the following in mind:

- Main trunk (leader) is 8–10 feet high with an open center above.

- Lowest branch is 24–48 inches from the ground.

- Five to twelve scaffold branches spaced 18–24 inches apart vertically along the trunk..

- Scaffold branches should form two tiers, each having four to six branches.

- The crotches of the scaffold branches should form 40- to 90- degree angles with the trunk.

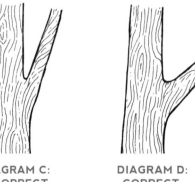

DIAGRAM C:
INCORRECT

DIAGRAM D:
CORRECT

OPEN-CENTER SYSTEM

Peach, apricot, nectarine, and sour cherry trees respond best to this system.

There should be no vertical trunk (central leader) in these trees.

- A single trunk is 18 to 30 inches in height, and this means a new tree should be cut down to this height either just before or after you plant.

- Three to four scaffold branches should be located 6–8 inches apart vertically near the top of the trunk and kept about equal size by pruning. Try to prune at a point where you will leave branches or buds that will become branches pointing in all four directions around the tree.

- All scaffold branches should form a crotch angle of 40- to 90- degrees with the trunk. (See Diagrams C and D.) Space as uniformly as possible from each other.

This is sometimes called a "vase" tree with an open center. It is an ideal shape to let in the sunlight and allows for easy care and harvesting of the fruit. A visit to commercial orchards will provide a great example of this type of pruning system.

Bonus Box: Branch spreaders made from wood or metal may be useful in achieving wider angles in young and pliable trees.

Thanks to Jerry Goodspeed, Weber County USU Extension Agent for much of the information on pruning fruit trees.

Ornamental Shrubs

ROSES

Roses are the Queens of the garden. Thought by some to be too finicky and demanding, they grow with little more care than any other flowering shrub. Once you meet a few basic requirements, they can last for your lifetime. Even before planting you need to select a good rose plant. First and foremost, always buy a Grade #1 plant. There will be many "sale" roses to tempt you to save money but they most often lead to disappointment. Those cheap (well, less expensive at the very least) roses are probably Grade #1½ or even Grade #2. It signifies that they have less

vigorous growth and weaker and thinner canes. You can let the color or fragrance entice you to a particular rose but just put it down and back away if it isn't Grade #1. Honest, you can find that same color or fragrance somewhere else in a better grade.

To get the best flowers from your rose once it's in the garden, the bush should have at least six hours of direct sunshine. Even knowing that, I planted about a dozen mini roses near my front door on the north side of my home. That area is lucky to get five hours of direct sun, and after that they are shaded by a huge Austrian Pine. I haven't told my little roses that all their blossoms are going against the prevailing opinions, and I don't let them read any books that could burst their bubble either.

Granted, the first flush of flowers from my mini roses is abundantly lovely, and then they go quickly to a sparse version of their former glory. But they brighten that little area next to the sidewalk and as long as they think they can, I'll let them grow there.

ROSE PRUNING

Rose pruning is a spring-thing in the Intermountain West. Middle of March usually finds the buds along the rose canes (stems or branches) starting to swell. When the buds get about ¼-inch long, it should be about time to go find the pruning shears. Be forewarned—when completed there will be very little left of your huge rose bush. The exceptions to the following pruning guidelines include mini roses, climbing roses, and most shrub or hedge roses. Those *included* in the guidelines are:

- **Hybrid Tea:** Generally 3 to 5 feet tall, with roses borne on single stems.
- **Floribunda:** Generally 2 to 4 feet tall, the flowers borne in clusters, looking like groups of bouquets on the bush.

- **Grandiflora:** Usually the tallest of the rose bushes, some will get as tall as 7 feet in one season. The individual flowers resemble Hybrid Tea but grow in clusters.

These guidelines are the roughest of the rough and are offered with apologies beforehand to my rosarian friends.

Preferably with long-handled pruners (they will lessen the blood loss—yours), start the procedure by:

1. Cut every cane down to 3 feet tall.

2. Now, reach into the center of the bush and cut any dead cane down as close to the ground as you can.

3. Any living (usually green in color) cane that is smaller than a pencil should be cut off, either to the ground or back to the next larger cane.

4. If there are more than seven or so canes left on the bush, remove three or four of the oldest, woodiest ones right to the ground. If the rose bush has still many, many canes remaining after the oldest are cut, remove 1 out of every five remaining canes starting with oldest (biggest) woody ones. With some good fortune, you should now be looking at five to seven strong, green canes, each around 3 feet tall.

5. You can stop right there, put the pruners away, and go find the Band-aids for a little medical clean-up after your "war with the roses."

6. One more step is optional: cut another foot off the canes of the Grandiflora and Hybrid Tea roses, making them roughly two feet tall. This usually makes for fewer but larger roses.

PRUNING OTHER FLOWERING SHRUBS

Many flowering shrubs have finished putting on their show of early flowers around the end of May. Forsythia (the early yellow one), Lilacs, Snowball bushes, and Mock Orange (the one that is white and drifts its perfume a block away), need to be pruned within about four to six weeks after the last petals fall. Shortly after that the shrub gets right to work producing the next year's flower buds.

Pruning needs to be done in those few weeks right after bloom or you will be cutting off all the flower buds that would have given you the colorful spring greeting you were hoping for. Fall pruning makes for no spring blooming for the spring blooming shrubs.

If you would like a shrub that blooms later in the season, consider planting a Rose of Sharon. The flowers resemble the tropical hibiscus although much smaller. Both have colorful petals that surround a funny little pokey out part of the flower right in the middle that looks like a little white dowel. The family resemblance is striking but not surprising—they are close relatives in the hibiscus family. Bloom time is late summer or early autumn. Another late bloomer is a Butterfly Bush. Both of these shrubs should be pruned after they bloom or very, very early in the spring.

PLANTING SHRUBS

Planting shrubs is done in the same way as planting trees. (See page 37.) Watering should be consistent during the first couple of years after planting, once every two weeks or so depending on the heat and natural precipitation. After the third year, woody shrubs other than roses may need no more than a once-a-month deep soaking. Far more shrubs are lost to overwatering than ever thirsted to death.

> **Bonus Box:** Great shrubs for hedges are Shrub Roses, Privet, Boxwood, Euonymous, Lavender (short hedges!), Barberry, Juniper, or Tallhedge Buckthorn.

GENERAL CARE OF SHRUBS

Unless shrubs show signs of iron deficiency or reduced flowers and lighter green of the leaves, there is no need for extra fertilizing after planting.

One extra effort that will be appreciated by all shrubs is a weekly shower bath of plain hose water. Hit both the top and bottom sides of the leaves and both dust and some offending insects and mites will be removed.

Flowers

ANNUALS

Frost can linger this time of year, and with it the danger of losing your newly-planted flowers. The average last frost date varies from state to state, county to county, and even town to town. Once you have learned that date, try to remember what

"average" means. Two weeks earlier than that average date is just as likely for a frost as two weeks later. In Zone 5 the average date might be around the middle of May. Since that usually coincides with Mother's Day, some gardeners use that as the signal date Vrooom . . . gardeners, start your trowels! However, gardeners who have lost every blooming annual they planted on that date three years running usually decide Memorial Day is a somewhat safer signal date.

For many years I would buy the flats of flowers for my mother's garden for her Mother's Day present, but we wouldn't plant them until Memorial Day. My job was to pull the weeds, prepare the soil, get the plants, plant the flowers, and water them. My little mom's job, self-selected, was to stand over me with Dad's large golfing umbrella and provide shade until the job was done. We made a great team.

SELECTING ANNUAL FLOWERS

It seems like selecting the flats of flowers should be a straightforward procedure. But there are hidden problems that can pop up and plague your best-planned flower display. The first problem is all that color! Whew, rainbow-overload! What's the problem with that, you say? It's that the strongest, healthiest bedding plants are usually the ones with *no* color showing yet. They are short, stocky plants and loaded with buds, but very few open flowers. Try choosing the color by looking at the full blooming flats but then select a flat of the same flower variety further back on the shelf that is just in bud, but with no blooms.

Being seduced by those glorious marigolds, petunias, and geraniums can be the ruination of a great season. The difficulty *here* is that you may be blessed with all the cool shade in the world but with no more than an hour of direct sun on any of your flowerbeds. Shady areas just won't do for the sun-loving plants. And nothing will raise the drooping heads of marigolds, petunias, or geraniums again, nor convince them they were brought to your garden to bloom if you plant them in such a location.

Sunny gardens can create the same problem but with a reverse cause. Of course, bright sun shines all day on the gardens of people who fall in love with hostas, ferns, and tuberous begonias—all shade-loving plants. Sadness falls like a sack of potting soil when *those* plants turn into brown-edged crispy critters in two days and dead inside two weeks because of the intense sunshine.

The lesson to learn here is the necessity of reading the plant labels before selecting the plants for your flower garden.

- **Full Sun:** Full sun means direct sunlight for at least 8 hours.*

- **Partial Sun/Partial Shade:** Partial shade means filtered shade from a tree or shrub the entire day or shade from early afternoon on.

- **Full Shade:** Full shade means dense shade as cast by a wall or fence for eight or more hours a day and filtered shade during other hours.

   *Warning: Full sun in Des Moines, Iowa or Portland, Oregon is different than full sun in St. George, Utah. Humidity and altitude also come in to play when choosing the site for your flowers. In high-altitude, low-precipitation areas even sun-loving plants appreciate shade in the hot afternoon.

FORMULA FOR PLANTING ANNUALS

As a general rule, most people plant too few annuals in a flower bed so when the flowers grow, bare patches of ground show in between. To achieve a beautiful and full effect, a good formula to follow is to figure the approximate square footage of the flower bed, then multiply by two. That will be the number of flowers you will need to purchase for that bed. When going to the nursery to select plants, have that number in mind as you select the plants you wish to buy. Mix a variety of different sized plants, types, and textures together to add interest and variety to the bed.

PLANTING ANNUALS

The tops *and* bottoms of annual flowers need attention during the planting process. Dig the hole twice as wide as the little mass of roots. Give the roots a ruffling—they should be "sticky-outy" instead of a tight little bundle. Water the hole before you place the plant. Fill the holes and let the water seep into the soil. If it doesn't seep, but rather creates little muddy swimming holes, review the section on improving your soil.

Plant by putting the little plant in the hole to the same depth it was growing in the plastic nursery container, pat the soil down into the hole, and water again.

FLOWERING PERENNIALS

Treatment for the tops of the plants can be a touchy subject. To encourage the plants to be at their blooming best for the entire season, any existing flowers should be pinched off. Ouch! I know — you chose those particular plants because they were *so* colorful and bright. Should you get brave enough to pinch or clip off those flowers, in a week to ten days you will be rewarded with many more blossoms. For the more reluctant and timid among you, may I recommend a "reciprocal pinch agreement" with a neighboring gardener? Somehow, it seems to hurt less if you are pinching *someone else's* petunias instead of your own.

While you are planning and planting your annual flower garden, give a moment's thought about adding a veggie or two. Carrots make a lovely fern-like edging. Rhubarb chard is stunning with deep red stalks and wavy deep green leaves. The smaller pepper plants look like little carnival attractions later in the season with their green, red, and yellow peppers dangling from the stems. Even a Jack-B-Little pumpkin winding its way thru' the bed is an eye-catcher come October.

Flowering Perennials—Spring Bulbs

Of all the bright spring flowers, those springing forth from fall-planted bulbs are among the easiest to grow and fall in love with. Tiny early flowers seem to be the little straw that breaks the winter's back. Little crocuses could be greeting you as early as the first of March if fall planting went well.

Rock garden tulips and grape hyacinths join the crocuses in the early spring color brigade. Now you will see why they do best planted in little herds. A single crocus can literally be here today and gone tomorrow. If you looked the other way when you walked through the front door, you missed the whole show—and you'll need to wait an *entire year* to see them again. All these spring beauties bloom once and then go dormant and disappear from view. However, if it is a herd of fifteen or more crocuses grouped in one little place, at least some of them will hang around long enough to get your attention.

As the rest of the bulb-brigade comes into flower, the garden lights up like a party waiting to happen. All good things come to a close, however, and as the

flowers dry up, it's time to get out the scissors or pruners. Cut the flower stalk down as far as you can but don't cut back the green leaves. The longer you can leave them there, the stronger the flowers will be the next spring. Green leaves produce the "food" that is stored in the underground bulbs. Enough stored food triggers the formation of the flower bud for next spring's display. When the leaves are totally dried out, or so tacky and shredded you can't stand looking at them any longer, clip the leaves off at ground level.

EARLY-BLOOMING PERENNIALS

About the time the bulbs are in full swing you will start seeing the signs of other perennials beginning to grow. Don't be too anxious to remove all the mulch from these perennial plants. Bulb foliage is tough, but late hard freezes can do some damage to late-blooming perennials. By the time the daffodils are all in bloom, it is usually time for the full garden cleanup to begin. The new shoots coming from the perennials are very fragile, so don't get too vigorous with the raking. After the garden and winter debris is removed, a generous addition of organic mulch will make the gardens look fabulous. Mulch will also perform the other jobs it does so well including reduction of weed growth and retention of moisture in the soil.

Early blooming perennials like Basket of Gold, Rock Cress, Candy Tuft, or Creeping Phlox need a good haircut once the flowers have faded. Nothing technical here—simply grab a handful of stems, gather them in your hand, and whack off the stems just below where the flowers grew. Usually this reduces the size of the plant nearly in half. That's all the care they need until next spring.

Deadheading—the process of trimming off flowers after they have finished being pretty—leads to many perennials rewarding your effort by blooming over and over again. This doesn't happen so much with the early bloomers, but many of the plants flowering from May on will appreciate the treatment and will show it by blooming again. The little early-blooming guys just smile in their little plant way and promise to strut their stuff again next spring. To keep all of the plants looking neat and tidy after deadheading, cut the flower *stalk*, as well as the spent flower, down to the next set of leaves. That eliminates the "bunch of old sticks" appearance.

June, July,
and August

JUNE, JULY, AND AUGUST

MINI-GLOSSARY

Backfill	To refill a trench or other excavation with the soil dug out of the hole and/or soil amendments.
Cane berries	Berries that grow on long stems coming out from ground level.
Dog days	The period of time between July 3 and August 11.
Hardened off	Gradually expose the tender plants to wind, sun, and rain and toughen them up.
Intensive Planting	A way to grow plants by placing them close together in a garden. Usually done in raised beds rather than in rows.
Recurrent	Blooming more than one time during the growing season.
Shoot (aka watershoot, watersprout)	New growth on a tree growing straight up, often from the middle of a branch where nothing had been growing before.
Stone fruit	Fruit that has a pit in the center.
Sucker	New, straight growth coming from the bottom of the tree, usually originating from the roots.

MUSINGS

In June, with the roses blooming, the geraniums coming into full glorious color, and nearly every plant sporting a lovely color of green in one shade or another, it is hard to remember that those dog days are just around the corner. Seems like "dog days" should have something to do with your collie or the neighbor's chocolate Labrador, or at least a foot-long barbeque component, doesn't it? However, we need to look to the sky for the dog connection. This is the season when the Dog Star, Sirius, rises in the morning with the sun. Ancient Romans believed this star added brightness and heat to our sun, and the result is felt during the hottest part of summer. The *Old Farmer's Almanac* lists the dog days of summer running from July 3 to August 11. So don't blame a yapping Sheltie for the term dog days, just thank the heavens for the long, hot days.

During these months, with Memorial Day just behind us and the Fourth, and in Utah the Twenty-fourth, of July enticing us just days ahead, our thoughts can start to stray away from the garden. Holidays and long weekends are terrific for the gardeners but can really lay a garden low. And if it weren't enough to be left on its own for days or weeks at a time, many areas are still panting from the dog days when they get clobbered with heavy rain and hailstorms. In five minutes a promising garden can be tattered and shredded beyond recognition.

When the storm passes, the corn is now horizontal instead of vertical and the beets look like green confetti, many gardeners are ready to throw in the trowel. But take heart—much can be salvaged.

Stand the corn back upright, add soil to the base, and tamp in gently. There! All is right in the corn patch. Crops that are more leaf than stem just need a little encouragement. *What* crops? you may ask as you survey the piles of green leaf confetti.

With a little trimming, some additional fertilizer, and more mulch, most homeowner's gardens will recover and go on to produce bountifully. A few words of praise won't hurt either, like: "Oh, aren't you looking good!" or, "All those new little leaves. I'm so proud of you." Repeated up and down the rows or around the raised beds, these words *will* help raise their drooping heads again!

Summer Lawns

MOWING

Mowing is the chore of choice for many male gardeners. As a female gardener, I find it satisfying as well. Green little blades of grass all standing at attention, perfectly matched flattop haircuts lined up together. Fine and dandy, but I can take it or leave it.

But for some gardeners, this *is* the garden. And my experience is that a lawn compulsion is most often a "Man Thing." Not exclusively maybe, but darn near. The weekend for men is always mandatory mowing, edging, adjusting sprinklers, and raking up or blowing away any leaf that dares fall on the *lawn*. Trees? They figure trees are good for shading bluegrass turf. Shrubs? Those are only the green, lumpy things alongside the lawn—usually seen as something that pokes them in the eye when mowing. Flowers? Something taking up ground space that once was lawn. Narrow view perhaps, but it is one valued most by the "Lawn Folk."

Whether maintenance is a compulsion or a pleasant chore, the resulting well-cared-for lawn is quite pretty. Pretty that is, until mid-July through August. For the cool season, grasses would rather just go dormant, become the color of straw, and sleep until September, thank you very much. At least for the gardener that grows a warm season grass like Zoysia grass, your lawns are finally looking great! In areas that are best for cool season grasses though, those warm season grasses don't green up until late June and they go back to straw-colored dormancy by early September. So try not to succumb to the siren song of the "perfect" lawn grass as seen on the back of the Parade section of the newspaper. The crime of omission is committed there. Nearly no water needed or morning, hardly need to ever mow . . . all true as long as where you live has nothing even akin to a real winter. Remember—you have been warned.

FERTILIZING

For the health of your cool season grass (usually bluegrass or a fescue variety) hold off on the fertilizer during the hottest months. Fertilizing in July and August just adds insult to injury by *making* the little blades grow faster so you can cut their heads off more often.

WATERING

Even if you have a so-so attitude towards grass, your cool season lawn *can* still hold its own with the Lawn Folk down the block. Okay, maybe you don't sharpen your lawnmower blade every other week. You don't use two mowers, reel and rotary blade, to get the perfect texture. Top dressing is something you think goes on a salad. And edging the lawn gets done twice a year, whether it needs it or not. Maybe you don't even view every dandelion as a personal attack on your signature green space. But with the proper mowing height, watering depth, and good placement of your lawn, your name will be right up there on the "Making our Neighborhood Look *Good*" list.

The training of a happy summer lawn should have started back in March when the roots were encouraged to grow deeply. If it didn't happen then, don't try to enforce the training program during these hot, dry months. That rigorous regime of waiting to water until the grass is grievously stressed would be a bad idea this time of year. The combination of high temperatures, wind, very little precipitation, and little or no humidity can be nearly lethal to a lawn. This is especially true of a bluegrass lawn.

So concentrate on (1) mowing correctly; (2)

watering infrequently but sufficiently long to have the water penetrate at least 6–8 inches; and (3) shaking your fist and, if necessary, cursing the weeds.

WEEDS

Oh, the weeds kind of sneak up on you and come in full battle array during the hot months. Many of the weeds didn't even germinate and start growing until a week into the real beginning (June 21) of summer. Here they are: the dandelions, thistle, puncture vine, chickweed, purslane, crabgrass (the *real* crabgrass), knotweed, oxalis, Field Bindweed, and spurge brigade. Their armor, an assortment of characteristics, such as 17-foot deep roots, seeds that stay ready to germinate for half a century, pokey parts that draw blood and pop bicycle tires, little seed pods that spit seeds 5 or 6 feet away, and get away vehicles shaped like little miniature umbrellas or parachutes.

Gardeners love to hate weeds and seek to destroy them with a vengeance. Chemical warfare has been raised to new heights in this arena. After all, every single weed is a personal attack on the "Lawn Folks" image, and the "Look-Good" list keepers frown on the unkempt lawn.

For the sake of all other living creatures in the environment, a gentler, if not kinder, approach is needed. Dogs, cats, and children play on these lawns. Little bare feet and paws are exposed to the chemicals spewed out to do battle against the monstrous weed attack. Even when you follow the label directions to let the toxic stuff dry sufficiently, it lingers on. Exposing living things to the possibility of absorbing those chemicals through their skin is a rather thoughtless act.

To sum up, cool season grass growers, remember to mow long and water deeply, add core aeration and fall fertilizing as compliments to spring root training and you'll be rewarded with the kind of lawn you always wanted—dark green, and luxurious.

Vegetables

PLANTING—EARLY AND LATE

June is great for planting all but the earliest cool season crops. And a mid-August planting gives you a chance at an additional fall harvest of those early crops. Second week in August, because you have already prepared your soil (right?), is the time to put in peas, green onions, spinach, lettuce, radishes, chard, kale, short season cucumbers, and beets. Early hard frosts will cut short your harvest in some years, but the ground was probably lying fallow after pulling the dried peas, lettuce, radishes, and spinach from the first of the growing season anyway so not much lost.

> **High on a Mountain Tip:** Cool weather crops will grow longer into the summer months in a high altitude climate. As soon as hot weather hits, plants like lettuce will quickly bolt to seed and become bitter to the taste. This will take longer at a higher altitude. Providing a little shade to these cool-weather plants will prolong the harvest.

> **High on a Mountain Tip:** Many fruits and vegetables taste better when grown in a cooler climate. An example is that the mere mention of "Bear Lake Raspberries" makes your mouth water—they grow best in a cooler climate.

PLANTING MELONS AND WINTER SQUASH

Seed packages talk of planting these seeds in a "hill." But don't envision or try to create a mini mountain. A hill of beans, or squash or melons, really means a few seeds grouped closer together than normal. And sometimes it helps to make a small mound (two inches high at most) to mark the spot where they are planted. To get a good reliable harvest of the long-season melons and squashes, it is a good idea to buy these as transplants rather than direct seeding in the ground anyway.

You can create a little mound for your plants if you want to, but it isn't necessary. Melons and squash *really* do not appreciate their roots being disturbed, so slip them very carefully from the little pots they are in, and backfill gently when you plant them.

If you are trying to grow melons in an area that is just marginally warm enough, you can increase the chances of actually getting them to ripen before frost by heating the soil with either clear or black plastic mulch before planting and then keeping the mulch in place during the entire growing season. You can plant right through the plastic by cutting an "X" or a "T" and folding back the "flaps" and digging the hole. After planting and watering well, fold the flaps back around the plant and leave the plastic in place the entire season. Tomatoes, peppers, and eggplants appreciate the extra warm soil too.

CORN

Corn, as a home garden crop, has a very small return for the space, water, and nutrients supplied by the gardener. My recommendation for newbies is to consider finding the local Farmer's Market or roadside stand as the best place to harvest your corn! Should

you still want to give "growing your own" a crack, here are just a few suggestions:

- Corn requires warm soil to germinate, so don't try planting early (Intermountain folks usually wait until after the first of June).
- Because corn is wind pollinated there is generally a better production of ears if you plant in blocks instead of long rows. (There are exceptions to every rule: my cousin got great production by planting little lines of 4 stalks each along a fence in her garden. There were flowering shrubs between every little line.)
- Water very consistently.
- Add an extra organic source of nitrogen fertilizer to the soil before planting, such as bat guano, blood meal, or fish meal. (Or even the fish heads and innards remaining after your last successful fishing trip.)
- Expect only one or two ears of corn per stalk.

Corn is one vegetable of which we *only* eat the seeds and that means if you are growing corn and don't have a couple of acres to plant with, pick only one kind of corn to grow. Cross pollination with a different variety usually results in what could, at best, be described as feed corn. Not concerned? Pigs and chickens like to eat feed corn. So plant one variety at a time or maintain distance of 100–200 feet between plantings.

OTHER VEGGIES

If you are just now jumping on the planting bandwagon, instructions for planting all the other vegetables can be found in the March, April, May section of this book.

WEEDS AND OTHER PESTS

Weeds begin to overtake all but the best-kept gardens by late summer. Because this can be so terribly discouraging, use mulch, mulch, and more mulch to keep the green scourge at bay. Sure, we may not win, but if we don't weaken and keep up the good fight, winter will soon rescue us! I just don't know how those year-round gardeners do it. I'm so ready to stop come the end of November, I can hardly wait. But in order to enjoy the wonderful season of fall gardening, gardens growing during these wonderful months should be allowed a little freedom to escape your complete control. A totally controlled garden negates the wonder of the continual change of growing things. Occasional weeds have a place in your garden. They feed and house the beneficial insects, provide nectar and pollen for the honey bees, and in some areas, even become a living mulch that helps reduce evaporation of water from the soil.

Before you think that Joy gave you permission to forget about weeding altogether, once again remember the gardener's saying, "One year seeding means seven years weeding." The best weed to pull is the tiny one. When you keep up with the little weeds, you won't let the beets, carrots, and potatoes that should have been on your table be swallowed up by the huge weeds.

PLANT-EATING PESTS

Weeds aren't the only things trying to swallow your produce during the summer. The Pest Most-Wanted list is beginning to fill up. And again, chemical warfare is often the knee-jerk reaction to something, *anything*, eating the leaves in the vegetable garden. Insecticides, the chemical kind, may not do any good because it may not even be an insect doing the damage!

"Know your enemy" is a good admonition to gardeners. Slugs and snails are voracious eaters and may well be the cause of your munched leaves. Since they are mollusks—more closely related to squids than insects—only a pesticide made for mollusks will kill them. The most widely used product, metaldehyde, is extremely harmful to cats, dogs, and kids. You can use an alternative product containing iron phosphate that won't harm anything but the slugs and snails. The main difference between a slug and a snail is that the slug doesn't have a shell.

To track down what is actually doing the damage often requires a nighttime forays into the garden. After dark, armed with a flashlight, you may spy the pest right in the act of munching.

Once the identity is determined, *then* you can decide on your next course of action. Sometimes that is no action at all! Nature has the ability to return balance to the garden if we haven't killed off the very creatures that would have taken care of the problem. Sadly, beneficial and predatory insects are more susceptible to chemical pesticides than the ones doing the damage.

One of the best deterrents for attacking insects is a very healthy plant. An unhealthy plant suffers from stress and is more susceptible to diseases *and* insects. Insects are actually *attracted* to a plant under stress. Reducing stress on a plant can only be done if you have identified the cause of the stress. Strangely enough, in a row of nearly identical plants, there may be only one or two that are having problems. Even plants that are close together may have different growing conditions. Determine if watering is uneven, if the plants were planted too deep or too shallow, or if sunlight hits them differently. It takes up-close and personal contact with your garden to determine the cause of any problems. Don't be a "window gardener," gazing out on occasion and seldom setting foot in the garden at all. Even weeds look pretty good at a distance.

MISSED THE BOAT?

Not so! Some gardeners worry that if they missed the early, mid, and late *spring* planting time that the growing season is a lost cause until next year. Not so! June is a grand time for putting in most warm season crops. In years past if you missed the planting window of late May to early June, you were out of luck when you headed to the nursery to buy your tomato, pepper, melon, or squash plants. What remained were pitiful shadows of their former selves. Having way outgrown their little plastic container, some veggies were even trying to set fruit before moving on to the Great Compost Bin in the sky. And it is tempting to want to give the little orphans a home in your garden. Don't do it. The stress has accumulated to an overwhelming degree and those plants won't go on to give you anything but grief.

That's the way it *used* to be. Now savvy professionals realize that planting can, should, and often by necessity, must continue later into the season. Results? Fresh little transplants straight from the greenhouse to you, even as late as July. Can't tell if they are stunted little old plants or just young fresh ones? Pop one out of the pot and check the roots. A tangle of white, nearly solid roots with hardly a particle of soil between them indicates a way overdue trip to the bin. If the roots are visible but there is a lot of fairly loose soil in the pot—bingo—you have yourself a transplant!

PLANTING LATE

The intense sun during the summer months can kill young plants as quickly and surely as a deep late frost.

Choose a cloudy day, if possible, for your planting. Place plants out in the evening so there are at least a few hours for them to get ready for the onslaught of the wide wonderful world that is your garden. Plants *can* get sunburned—the leaves usually turn white. A piece of wood or cardboard propped up as a tent for a few days on the south/north sides of the young plant can prevent the damage.

By the time you get around to planting tomato plants later in the season, even young and otherwise healthy ones may have grown quite long and spindly. I've seen the poor young things out in a garden waving in the wind like little green flags of surrender. The ones that don't just drop over from wilt sometimes snap in two from even a slight breeze. There is such a cool remedy for this pitiful demise: *a trench!*

Dig a slanted trench, or even a deeper hole than usual, and bury the tomato plant up to 4 or 5 inches from the top of the plant. It may be necessary to pinch off the lower leaves so that just the stem underground. Gently bend the stem so it is pointing straight up and fill in the trench or hole. Even young tomato plants that are less than eight inches tall will benefit from stripping the lower leaves and planting them with only 4 inches or so left above ground. The really lanky ones benefit from the slanted trench approach. Tomato plants will then form roots all along the buried stem. This technique is only used on tomato and pepper plants.

Most vegetable plants should be planted just a little deeper than they were growing in the pots. Be extra gentle when you take cucumbers, melons, and winter squashes out of their nursery pots. They respond poorly to ruffled roots. Make sure the soil in the pots is very moist and water the garden area thoroughly the day before planting. Turn the pot on its side and carefully pull it away from the plant. Softly place the transplant down in the hole and backfill with the soil you removed from the hole. Because these plants have relatively large leaves, they will suffer from water stress very easily. Be sure to keep an eye on them. Check every day to see if they need watering. Poke down in the soil just outside the area of the roots and feel if the soil is moist. It is possible to drown the plants with kindness by overwatering. Water only if the first inch of soil feels dry. The direct sun may cause them to wilt—again because of their large leaf surface—so a tent will be most appreciated by the little guys for a week or so.

WATERING

The roots of the already growing transplants are in just that tiny little area at the base of the plant. Water must be given often and close to the plant. Later, as the plant grows, the roots will range widely and it won't be so critical to get water right to the tiny piece of soil near the stem. Soil in the seed-planted area needs to be kept moist until and after the seedlings appear. Don't neglect the watering chore or you will be greeted by wilted or even dead little plants, and you won't even *see* the seedlings that died before they hit the surface of the soil.

As veggies continue to grow, adding mulch over the growing area will reduce the number of times per week you need to water. There are a few crops that only respond with vigorous growth if you water heavily and often. Corn needs consistent water so it is never left to grow in dry soil. Melons put out more and larger fruit when they don't experience drought. Winter squash, including pumpkins, need both water and extra fertilizer to grow to a very large size. Potatoes grow very "knobby" if the soil dries com-

pletely between waterings. Lettuce gets bitter without consistent soil moisture. Radishes become Atomic Fireball hot when growing in drier soil. Cucumbers can develop bitterness from inconsisten watering. Tomatoes and peppers can develop blossom-end rot from drastically fluctuating soil moisture.

Even without glaring problems from lack of or inconsistent watering, all produce need sufficient water to be at their prize-winning best. Make your choice, but remember why you decided to grow veggies in the first place. Taste and nutrition probably ranked near the top. Don't shortchange yourself or your plants—water wisely.

FERTILIZING

Rich soil with abundant organic matter needs no extra fertilizer to nourish plants. Produce will be higher in vitamins and amino acid content if no extra chemical fertilizer is added to the soil. Studies have shown that even mineral content in produce grown in organic soil is higher. And to protect your garden plants from diseases and pests, keep in mind that excess nitrogen fertilizer will lower a plant's resistance to those invaders. Even flavor and taste is improved when there is no extra inorganic nitrogen added and only organic fertilizers are used.

There are some natural additives to jump start the natural reduction of organic matter into available nutrients. Bat guano and cottonseed meal are good sources of nitrogen. If you have added organic matter that still looks like leaves, grass clippings, or lettuce leaves, there will be a need for a little extra nitrogen. For most crops, herbs, and flowers, an all-purpose organic fertilizer should do the job.

HARVESTING

Corn

Fresh corn is an absolute treat—and with the super sweet varieties it almost qualifies as a dessert!

Picking corn is easy—grab the husk-covered ear and twist it off the stalk. Being able to tell if it is ripe is another skill all together. Peel back the husk a little—just a little, because you may need to leave that ear on the stalk a while longer—to expose the little kernels. Poke one with a fingernail and if juice squirts out it's time to pick. If the little kernel still has the silk attached or is rather flat instead of plump, you need to wait a couple of days. If the kernel is big and tightly packed against the other kernels AND when you poke with a fingernail it

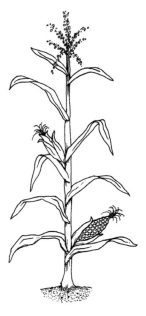

High on a Mountain Tip: In areas with shorter growing seasons, you may want to take a risk and plant your corn in May—but be prepared to cover up the entire corn row if those tender green shoots are above ground and it freezes. One such high-country gardener plants corn in early May with the thought that if it freezes, he can start over, but if the corn makes it, he will be that much further ahead! It is easier to cover a row of corn that is only 2–3 inches high in the spring, compared to covering corn that is 6-feet tall in the fall and almost ripe.

just dents in, sorry Charlie, you waited too long.

With the newly developed super sweet varieties of corn, you can actually put the ears in the fridge for a day or two and it will still be perfectly sweet and ready to eat. In the "olden" days, it was often said that the way to have a perfect ear of corn on the cob was this—get a big pot of water and bring the water to a boil. Only after it's boiling do you go to the garden to pick the corn. Then you start running back to the kitchen, but if you fall down on the way by the time you get up, the corn is too old and you'll need to go back and pick fresher ears!

Tomatoes

For an ear-to-ear grin and dancing exuberance nothing can beat your first homegrown tomato. If you chose a tomato variety with a fairly short growing season you can aim high and hope for tomatoes by the Fourth of July. Don't be dismayed if you must settle for fried *green* tomatoes on the Fourth, it *is* more likely in most gardens. Fried green tomatoes are a treat, but the two stages of ripeness are certainly not interchangeable.

To maximize the enjoyment of your first ripe tomato, try attaching a salt shaker to a bamboo teepee right out among the tomato plants. Wipe the tomato lightly with your sleeve, lick one side, apply the salt (you lick so the salt will stick!) and bite in like you would a ripe apple.

Extra Bonus Box: Should you find a salt shaker with a waterproof lid like Tupperware makes, devise a way to hang it in your tomato patch. Maybe you just went out to pull a few weeds or grab a pepper for your salsa, but ah-ha, you spot a perfect tomato. No need to delay slurping it down if your handy-dandy salt shaker is right there at your elbow.

Holy moley—a flavor explosion in your mouth! Everyone deserves that indescribable experience at least once in their life. You'll never view tomatoes the same way after that. The only downside is that you'll never be able to enjoy off-season grocery store tomatoes in quite the same way again. Sigh. But summer will come again next year!

Warning: Overripe tomatoes leave a lot to be desired. They are soft and lacking in flavor. Tomatoes will continue to ripen after you pick them, so if you're going to be gone for a while, it's better to pick them slightly under ripe, or even slightly green and let the tomatoes ripen on a counter rather than let them get mushy soft.

Fruit

THINNING

Apples and pears ought to be thinned to 4–6 inches apart sometime during June. There is usually a period called June drop when the little apples that didn't get completely pollinated just fall off the trees. Nothing is wrong with the trees or the apples, but it is a good signal that it's time to work on thinning the rest of the fruit.

Peaches will drop the extra fruit too, but I always speed up the June drop process with my peaches. I grab hold of a couple of the branches and shake the

Joy's Favorite Fried Green Tomatoes

1 lb. green tomatoes (4 medium)
3 Tbsp. flour
3 Tbsp. grated Parmesan cheese
1 Tbsp. sugar *
2 tsp. (or so) salt
⅛ tsp. pepper
1 egg
2 Tbsp. water
4 cups bite-sized crispy corn squares, crushed = 1¼ cup (could use bread crumbs)

* If less tart tomato flavor is desired, sprinkle slice lightly with a little extra sugar

1. Combine flour, cheese, sugar, salt and pepper; set aside. Beat egg and water; set aside. Cut tomatoes in ¼-inch slices.

2. Dip each green tomato slice in flour mixture to coat both sides.

3. Dip in egg and then into cereal crumbs to coat thoroughly.

4. Allow slices to dry slightly while heating enough oil to cover bottom of frying pan.

5. Fry until browned, turning once About 3–4 minutes per side.

Recipe from the kitchen of Vaudis Campbell; used with permission.

bejeebers out of them. Down drop tons of little green peaches. *Then* I finish thinning the little fruit a week or two later until there are about 8 inches between the remaining peaches.

WEED AND MULCH

One of the worst weeds to let grow near fruit trees is lawn grass (remember the definition of a weed here!). Plan a way to put fruit trees in a separate growing area away from the lawn. Should you already *have* a fruit tree in the lawn—inherited from the previous owner I'm sure—remove the grass from the base of the tree out to a bare minimum of 18 inches, giving the tree a grass-free zone 3 feet wide. Don't give in to temptation and plant any pretty little flowers in that zone. Their watering needs are far too great to be living that close to a fruit tree.

When fruit trees live in their own space, away from the lawn, a deep layer of mulch will control any other weeds trying to grow nearby. Weeds aren't just unsightly—they use the water and nutrients the trees need to grow and produce properly. A weed barrier of newspaper or commercial woven material can help control the weeds, but I don't recommend either around a tree that is growing in the lawn area. The barrier will not let excess moisture evaporate from around the base of the tree. It is an important consideration since it's likely that the lawn is being watered (*over*watered actually) far too frequently for the health of a fruit tree.

PRUNING

During these summer months, pear, apple, *and* plum trees tend to send out new shoots (branches) that grow straight up into the air. Sometimes these grow near the ground coming from around the trunk. Sometimes they burst straight up from the middle of

an older branch. The water sprouts on the branches can be easily taken care of in June or July by "thumb pruning." Put on a tough glove (I like a leather glove for this job), and then just rub the little starts off the branch! This works on the new shoots that started in the current year. If you let them get a full year old, you will need hand pruners to remove them. After a couple of years, they will be 8 feet tall growing right up through the middle of your tree and you will need loppers or a saw to cut them down.

Whether near the trunk or on the branches, when you remove these unwanted stems, cut them even with the branch or root where they are growing. If you leave a little stub or a stump, there will be several suckers growing from the same spot the next year.

June and early July is a good time to do light pruning to shape apple, pear, and other fruit trees. Pruning in June doesn't prod the trees into a lot of new growth like early spring pruning does. This is a good time to tweak the pruning already done by removing a few more branches that have decided to rub the shingles off the roof, scratch the window screens during a windstorm, or poke somebody in the ear every time they walk by. Remember, no stubs or stumps left after the cut. To make sure any light pruning is done correctly, check out the spring section for correct pruning techniques.

WATERING FRUIT TREES

Fruit trees don't demand a lot of water. After the second season, one good soaking twice a month through July will be sufficient. When the fruit begins to enlarge and ripen, fruit trees and grape vines need more consistent watering but once a week is usually enough even then. Peaches and nectarines will develop stronger flavor if you stop watering for a couple of weeks before they are ripe.

PESTS

Stone fruit trees can be attacked by a few different pests. The one that has the potential to do the most damage is the Peach Tree Borer. This clear-winged moth lays her eggs on the bark of a tree, and when the egg hatches out the tiny caterpillar "bores" in through the bark. This is where the damage is done, not the hole in the bark but the burrowing that the larvae do just *under* the bark. It eats the thin layer of living tissue that grows the new wood (cambium layer), as well as the conductive tissue that moves water, nutrients, and "food" up and down the tree.

Sometimes you see a glob of clear amber-colored ooze coming from a little hole. This is usually an exit hole and signals that the larva completed its lifecycle and has emerged as an adult. This "glob" is a symptom called *gummosis*. If you spot the gummosis low on the trunk, it may well signal a borer has been doing damage to the tree. But this can also be a sign that other damage has occurred to the bark. Whacking with a lawnmower, string trimmer, stick (kids do that sometimes, you know), or even winter damage will result in the same symptom. There are other pests (it could be kids again, climbing up in the branches this time) that damage branches up higher in the tree. Again you will see some gummosis but it won't be the Greater Peach Borer that was the cause. That borer only attacks the lower 15 or so inches of the trunk, and sometimes low enough to be just below the soil surface.

HARVESTING

Peaches

Sum, sum, sum, summer time! Harvest is the watchword of the day for fruit growers. And knowing when the peaches are perfectly ripe is an art. You must watch closely to spot when they begin to develop a little reddish blush and lose all the green color in their skin. Over in the next tree, robins and finches are keeping the same vigil. The race is on! Who will sense when the smooth juiciness has peaked in those lovely peaches? The birds will probably win. They have nothing else to do so they sit and sit and sit and wait until the perfect moment to swoop in and delicately peck away at the peach. And

the little peck marks always seem to be hidden on the side of the fruit that isn't clearly visible to the gardener. Since you had to be off doing whatever it was that you needed to be off doing when the alarm clock of ripeness rang, you missed the moment. With a large peach tree there is enough fruit to share with the birds, neighbors, and family so a little pecking on a few peaches isn't disturbing. That young peach tree carrying its first three peaches is another matter.

You diligently, although reluctantly, picked off the peaches that formed last year to give the tree time to get established. It is very hard on a little tree to try and ripen fruit and grow good roots at the same time. This year you thinned properly and there were three lovely, well-spaced peaches left. For two months you have watched their growing and subtle color change. "Soon," you thought, "I will have peach juice running down my arm while I savor the bite of my first ripe peach!" A check in the morning indicates that this will be the day. One extra warm day in the bright sun, and it will be harvest time!

Oh, the sadness! The disappointment! The anger . . . grrrrr! The birds ate the backsides of all three of your peaches. After briefly entertaining dark thoughts of the bird annihilation variety, you pick the three peaches anyway. Back in your kitchen you carefully remove the pecked-on part and slice the remaining three half peaches into a bowl. To share or not to share, that is the question. Never mind, the rest of the family just came home. . . and descended on your peach slices like hungry robins and finches!

There, left at the bottom of the bowl is one little golden slice of peach. You pop it quickly into your mouth and with your tongue gently push the fruit up against the roof of your mouth. Ahhhhh! For a brief second, the burst of juice makes you forget that you just enjoyed the sum total of the harvest of peaches for the entire season. But being a true gardener, your only thought is "Wait until next year. I bet I'll get a bushel!"

Cherries

Cherries come on quickly. One day, they're a light straw color with a pink blush and the next day the robins and finches ate them all! In fairness to robins and finches, other birds probably had a hand in the disappearance of the cherries. Sometimes all you see left in the tree are scruffy pits hanging by the pitiful little stems. Some folks decide to foil the

bothersome birds by draping netting over the trees. The net helps a little bit, but be warned—little birds can get their feet snared in the net and beat themselves to death trying to escape. If trying to explain that to a visiting grandson makes you get a little queasy, skip the net.

Other contraptions like old shiny CD's or strips of aluminum foil or plastic owls have been touted as effective bird scaring devices. And they work for maybe a day or so. Then one of the braver birds gets closer, closer, closer. Hmmmm, that owl didn't even move! And all your feathered friends move in for a feast. Try what you like—each method may give you a day or two more toward ripeness and your harvest.

Here along the Wasatch Front, homeowners might just as well call their cherry tree a "Bird Feeding Station" and be content. Every cherry will probably have a protein supplement in it anyway. A spray regimen needs to be consistently maintained every three to five days from the first turning of straw color to the day of red ripe in order to possibly be effective against the Western Cherry Fruit Fly. So how much could little flies eat anyway, you ask?

Perhaps we better define protein supplement: maggot worms in the cherries. See? A Bird Feeding

Station sounds better now, doesn't it? And it can make a good shade tree to boot.

Pears

Pears hang on until September to ripen in many parts of the country. Pears need to be picked before they are fully ripe to avoid the fruit from becoming gritty. Little cells called Stone Cells develop in tree-ripened pears and live up to their name by giving the pears a sandy gritty feel in your mouth. You should pick the pears when the green skin starts turning light green and has little teeny spots. The seed in a pear cut in half should be brown in color, not whitish to signal the right time to pick a green pear. Pick the pears; put them on a counter in the house, and in a few days they will be perfect. To slow the ripening a little, put them in the fridge. To really hurry them up, put the fruit in a paper bag and close the top of the bag. Pears, at the ripe stage, will give a little when you push on them.

HARVEST AFTER FROST

Grapes

Most apples and the purple concord grapes will benefit from a frost or two before harvesting, so wait until September even if they are looking ripe. More sugar develops after the cold weather hits them. Harvesting table grapes—those seedless red, black, or green ones—becomes another race against the birds. Vineyards will sometimes put each bunch in an individual paper sack once the grapes begin to enlarge. It's up to you, but remember the dangling dead bird before you place netting over the grapevines. My dad always said, "Grapes are the smartest fruit in the world—leave them alone and they turn into wine!" Actually, if you and the birds leave them alone, they turn into raisins!

Plums

With plums, it's easy to tell when they're ripe—either the birds ate half of each one, or they fell on the ground. Okay, it isn't quite that bad. At least plums are fairly easy to tell when it's time to pick them. Ripe plums are scrumptious, and a little squeeze will indicate a slight softness that signals eating time. If you pick one that isn't quite ripe, the sudden tightness of your jaw and squinching up of your face will let other people know that the plums haven't quite sweetened up yet.

Berries

Raspberries are at perfect eating stage when they just fall into your hand with the slightest touch. They leave behind a core when you pick them. Blackberries and their kin (boysenberries, dewberries, marionberries) pull off core and all. But if you want to eat them at their sweetest, just the slightest pull should release them into your fingers.

Blackberries should be thoroughly black and even starting to lose a little of the sheen on each berry. The tiniest tug should release them from the plant and let them fall into your hand. I hope that when you chose the blackberries you planted, they were a thornless variety. Now, I know the thorny kind often have the larger berries. But I've pushed my hand into a thorny blackberry bush to harvest those big beauties. The hand goes in quite easily, grasps the gorgeous fruit and then . . . yeow! The thorns are curved backwards so they only start to draw blood on the way *out* of the berry patch tangle. Choose for yourself, but again, you have been warned.

Strawberries are ripe when fully red. The more you pick, the more they produce. June bearers have ripe berries in a short three to four week period. Everbearers will give you enough for a treat through

119

most of the growing season, although the strawberry production slows way down in July and August. "Day neutral" strawberries stay in good production from June through early September. Every region of the country has varieties of strawberries that do best in that neck of the woods, so check with your local extension office or nursery for the varieties to look for in the spring.

Trees

ORNAMENTAL TREES

Ornamental trees generally need little care during the summer. A stray branch or two may need pruning but other than that, a deep watering every couple of weeks and removal of lawn or weeds that have begun to creep in around their base is about all they need.

STRESS DAMAGE

Insect pests attack the stressed trees first, so keep the following stresses to a minimum:

- **Insufficient water:** This can be a cumulative problem. One season with a lack of water adding to the next until there is a tipping point where insects or diseases move into the weakened tree.

- **Overwatering:** This can also be a gradual stress that finally results in a disease organism infecting the vulnerable parts of the tree, usually the crown or roots.

- **Overfertilizing:** When trees, or any other plant, grows excessive tender new shoots and leaves the tissue is thin and it is much easier for insects to munch away. Diseases, particularly fungal diseases, get a start on the succulent new growth much more easily than on plant tissue that is tough and thick.

- **Physical damage:** bark is like a person's skin. It prevents invasion from nasty beasties that cause internal diseases and damage. Any nick or cut in the bark of a tree will allow access to these potentially deadly organisms. (See Page 59 for Winter Damage and Page 47 for Mower Blight.)

Hot temperatures, especially when it is windy, will almost always lead to scorch on the leaves. Once you make sure the symptom isn't from too much water, there isn't anything besides the infrequent deep watering that you can do about it. If you see several lines of scorch that look like bathtub rings of browning on the edges of the leaves, it is most likely from hot and dry conditions. Additional water will not help and might lead to *over*watering and the development of crown or root rot. Always check the soil moisture before watering an ailing tree. Dig down with a trowel and see just how far down the soil is moist or dry. Dryness down more than 5 or 6 inches is an indication it's time for a deep soaking around the shrubs.

Ornamental Shrubs

PRUNING

Hedges can be pruned now, even if you did it early in the spring. Many types of plants can be shaped to form a hedge.

Trimming now won't stimulate new growth as it did in the spring and the hedge will stay looking neat and tidy longer. The bottom of a hedge should be kept wider than the top. This allows sun to hit the bottom leaves and keeps the lower branches from losing leaves and showing naked stems near the ground.

Rose of Sharon is a late-blooming shrub that begins putting on the flower display late in August, continues through most of September, and in some areas into early October in some areas. Pruning of this shrub can be done late in the fall after it stops flowering or early next spring before the new growth starts. When you see little swelling spots on the stem called buds, it means the plants are off and growing again. Try to prune before you see green leaves.

Roses are flowering shrubs that like a little rest during the later part of the summer. Deadhead the spent flowers and fertilize for the last time around the first of August. In September, you will enjoy a colorful display of all the recurrent blooming roses. Don't fertilize roses after August because new growth later in the season won't be hardened off sufficiently and will likely die back during the winter.

INSECT PESTS ON SHRUBS

Spider mites love the hot, dry, dusty summer weather. Nearly all ornamental shrubs can be bothered by these sucking pests. There is an extra good reason for not using a miticide (a poison that kills mites). These poisons will be more lethal to the good guy mites than the ones sucking the life out of your shrubs. Give the predatory (good guy) mites a head start on multiplying faster than the bad guy mites by washing the dust off the outer branches and leaves of your shrubs or bushes (a shrub is a bush by any other name; although most people seem to think shrubs grow bigger than bushes). The undersides of the leaves are where the damaging spider mites love to hide, so be sure to squirt from underneath as well as from above. The predatory mites are biding their time in the interior of the plant, and after the shower bath they will be out killing many of any remaining bad guys—usually at night, after sundown.

This time of year, little notches start showing up around the edge of many shrubs. It looks like someone with a steady hand used a little punch or pink-ing shears to scallop the leaves. The damage doesn't show up toward the middle of the leaf, just around the edges. Blame a root weevil, usually the Strawberry Root weevil or Black Vine weevil. The munching beetle comes out to eat in the middle of the night. If you find yourself up at around two or three in the morning with nothing else to do, you could go out a-hunting the wiley weevil. They are about 1/8 to 1/4 of an inch long and usually black. There are faint ridges along their back and they have a bit of a snout. If you spot one and knock it to the ground, it will give the best imitation of a dead bug you have ever seen. Even the six little legs kind of curl towards its belly.

Tap it, push it around with your finger, even pick it up, and it will stay still as death. Walk away or just turn your head for a second, and it will roll over and scuttle away. Try trapping them by sinking some small straight-sided jars in the ground up to the rim. Root weevils spend their days hiding under fallen leaves or other debris around the plants they munch on. Once active at night, they will fall into the jars and not be able to get out. Empty the little jars every few days and reposition them down in the holes.

The damage done to leaves is usually just cosmetic but the larvae, or weevil, form can do enough damage to roots to affect the growth of the plant. Trapping is about the only way to reduce their numbers.

DISEASES OF SHRUBS

Powdery mildew starts showing up during the hot part of the summer. It appears as a grayish dusty looking patch on leaves of many shrubs. Since it is a fungal disease there is no cure, but you can prevent much of the infection by spraying leaves every week or so with a solution of . . . milk! Yep, one part milk to nine parts water. Spray every few days to keep the problem under control.

Flowers

MULCH

All flower beds and individual flowering plants will survive the summer heat better with an application of mulch over the growing area. This is as true for the annual flower bed as it is for around your perennials. A 2- to 4- inch layer of mulch goes a long way toward making the beds and the flowers look their best. Mulch, as with molding around a window, covers a multitude of mistakes or problems, so be generous in your application of mulch. Bought by the bag or truck load, mulch can be spread directly on the soil or over some form of weed barrier to solve two problems at once.

DEADHEADING

Another way to keep your annual flowerbeds looking their best is to diligently cut off the spent flowers. It keeps the area from looking sort of tacky and triggers the formation of more flower buds to open later.

PERENNIALS

Perennials, with their waves of color, are the center of attention during the summer months. At least they will be if you remember to plant varieties that come into bloom at different times. Color waves are just that—sometimes the flowers are at the crest and add spectacular pizzazz in every corner of your garden and then ebb to nothing but green during the off-bloom time.

June is still a good time to plant in many areas. Like most plants, perennials will do best when not plunked out in the garden midday when it is hot and maybe windy as well.

Hold off until September if you can, rather than planting in July or August. You may relish the 100 plus degree days and bright sunshine, but that makes for a jarring introduction to your garden for new plants.

Deadheading will keep perennials blooming for the longest time possible. If you want some varieties to reseed for next year, leave the last flowers that start to form in August, September, and October, on the plant. That way the seeds mature and scatter about in your garden.

FERTILIZING

If you have been fertilizing monthly, make the first part of August the last application around your perennials. They need to start their natural process of slowing down growth and getting ready for the winter dormant season.

WEEDS

Weeds come into their glory during the hot months. Many have been waiting all year for this. Crabgrass is just such a weed. Although most wide-bladed, tall weedy-looking grasses that plague our lawns get called "crabgrass," the real thing only germinates in the summer and is killed by the winter freezes. If you have those nasty grasses in your lawn growing in April, it isn't crabgrass. Preventing the formation of seeds is the best way to prevent the annual invasion of these weeds.

- **Field Bindweed:** Commonly called "Morning Glory" in the west. There is nothing glorious about it. Seeds can live for up to 50 years in the soil.

- **Common mallow:** Has a deep taproot that can easily be pulled from moist soil. Has little fruit children call "cheesies."

- **Knotweed:** The plant forms a tough, wiry mat of stems and leaves. To differentiate from spurge, a broken stem does not produce a milky sap.

- **Dandelion:** Perennial that has an extensive taproot. Its yellow flowers can develop any time between March and November and are followed by fluffy seed heads which children love to blow scattering the seeds everywhere!

- **Quackgrass**: A creeping perennial, is a very aggressive grass and is considered a noxious weed in some states. Sometimes mistaken for the annual crabgrass.

- **Spurge:** Another creeper, but it's an annual. Only shows up when the weather gets hot. Shows milky sap when the stem is broken. Loves to live in the lawn.

FULL CIRCLE IN THE GARDEN

And now that completes the cycle—summer's passing brings us back to September. Here, again, is the New Year's beginning in your garden and garden to be. Take stock of what has, or maybe hasn't, happened and vow to *really* dig in this time. Perhaps even plant a tree against which you can measure a child's growth!

Karen and I can measure the passing of years in the recollection of previous gardens. And every year that garden led to thoughts of a way to make the next one even prettier, more productive, or both!

Gardens in September are as full of promise as anywhere on earth. Either the harvest is gleaming in the garden or gleaming in the dreams of the gardener. There is a little poem that most folks have probably only heard or read the second verse. Dorothy Frances Gurney penned these gentle thoughts:

So near to the peace of Heaven
That the hawk might nest with the wren,
For there in the cool of the even
God walks with the first of men.

The kiss of the sun for pardon,
The song of the birds for mirth,
One is nearer God's heart in a garden,
Than anywhere else on earth.

More than twenty-five years ago, I came across another stanza etched on a small stone block near Bull Bay, Anglesey in Wales. No one had been given credit, but I think the same love of a garden touched this author as well:

The dawn of the moon for glory,
The hush of the night for peace.
In the garden at eve, says the story,
God walks and His smile brings release.

Gardens have a way of letting the weight of your cares just melt out of your feet and soak into the soil. We believe a life among plants is a richer, fuller more compassionate life. Get to know the plants that give you life with their oxygen. Help your family realize that lettuce doesn't grow in the produce department. Learn to recognize the magnificent difference between plants that collect dust over the years and living plants that are always changing. Introduce your children to a vertical wooden pole that isn't meant to hold up utility lines. Trees are our friends! Get to know them; let them teach you the wonder of growing. These are the messages of our book.

We hope your heart leads you to a garden of your own. Then you too will feel the strength and comfort that comes from working with plants and soil. When you get to that garden, we also hope this book will become a source of information and encouragement. Remember, you *can* find joy in YOUR garden!

APPENDIX
ORGANIC GARDENING

INTRODUCTION

Gardeners often wonder exactly what "organic gardening" means. The answer to this is found in a broad spectrum of gardening choices, from simply choosing not to use any synthetic fertilizers or pesticides in the garden all the way to becoming a certified organic grower, which entails many strict rules and regulations. For most gardeners, it is enough to stay at the less technical end and choose to wisely manage their lawn and gardens using healthy, safe methods.

Some gardeners prefer to stay completely away from any synthetic chemicals in their entire yard, while others stay chemical-free only around the vegetables. Stepping away from the edibles, the second group may actually get a fiendish delight in attacking stubborn weeds with a quick and deadly spray of RoundUp.

It's ultimately up to you to decide how far into the spectrum you want to go. The purpose of this chapter is to provide some basic ideas on how to begin implementing natural practices in the garden.

ORGANIC SOIL

Organic gardening begins with the soil. As mentioned over and over, there is nothing better for the garden than to add organic material regularly. Not only does this improve the structure of the soil, but it adds a variety of nutrients that are taken up and used, creating very happy well-fed plants.

Many of the raw ingredients of organic matter are right at your fingertips. Grass clippings, vegetable scraps, fruit rinds, fall leaves, and plant debris are all ideal ingredients to turn into a rich compost to improve your soil. All this and more can go into a *compost bin* to be returned to your garden later as dark, earthy compost. If you add compost to your soil, you're already well on your way to growing a beautiful, healthy garden organically.

COMPOST AS FERTILIZER

Whoa! Did someone actually say the words "compost bin"? Yes! It really is a shame to have all those lovely ingredients available and not turn them into compost. Composting isn't a daunting task to be avoided at all costs. In fact, it's relatively simple, once the basics are understood and the rewards are great. When this nutrient-rich black gold is added into your garden, the need for fertilizer is greatly diminished. Not only that but it is a very responsible way to recycle your yard and kitchen wastes and an important step in reducing the volume of garbage sent needlessly to landfills.

The first step to composting is to understand the process. Composting is the transformation of organic materials through decomposition into a soil-like material called compost. Microorganisms such as bacteria and fungi do the work of transforming this raw material into compost. This process can happen quickly or over a longer period of time, depending on the effort and diligence of the gardener. A neglected pile of plant waste or manure will eventually turn into compost and is basically passive composting. Fast (active) composting can be achieved by manually speeding up the process.

STEPS TO SUCCESSFUL COMPOSTING

Provide a bin to contain the ingredients to be composted. This can be as simple and inexpensive as a bin (or series of bins), made from wood pallets, to the more expensive commercial composters. Two considerations are (a) it needs to allow air circulation; (b) it needs to be large enough for the composting process to take place yet small enough to allow air and water to penetrate easily.

- Build a compost bin or bins (3–4 feet square in size).

- Add a wide variety of materials to the compost pile. A mixture of green and brown plant debris works well together, as does wet and dry material. Green material is fresh from growing, literally green in color. Brown material is woody plant material or leaves and plant parts that have been dead for a while and have, surprise, turned brown! Add fruit rinds, vegetable scraps, leaves, manure from anything that doesn't eat meat (no cat or dog manure), and moderate amounts of shredded up newspaper. Don't add baked goods or anything with sugar, as that will attract rodents and flies. Don't add large sticks or items that will take a long time to decompose. When adding grass clippings, dry them out first so they don't clump together and just rot. Even weeds can even be added, but are best dried out first and used before they go to seed. Make sure the pile doesn't contain more than approximately 20 percent of any one

item. The smaller the pieces, the quicker the compost will be ready, so chop up the ingredients, if possible.

- Add a little soil or finished compost scattered over each 8–10 inch layer of raw material, to get the whole process started.

- Add enough water so that the pile is moist, but not dripping wet. This is easier if you moisten each "layer" as you build up the pile. Perform a "squeeze" test and if water drips out, it is too wet. If this is the case, add more dry ingredients. If too dry, sprinkle in more water.

- Turn the pile weekly using a shovel or a pitchfork. The idea is to mix the ingredients so everything on the drier top and sides eventually ends up in the middle of the pile, where the composting action takes place. Adding air through turning keeps the smell to a minimum. Composting does *not* stink—rotting stinks. If your pile or bin stinks, it is rotting, not composting.

- Keep adding new ingredients.

- Compost is finished when it is dark, crumbly, and has a good earthy smell. None of the ingredients should be recognizable.

- If large pieces remain in the finished compost, sift them out with a screen.

- Add compost to garden soil as needed.

Some people like to have a series of three bins—one to hold finished, ready-to-use compost, one that is empty and one that is full of a variety of compost ingredients in progress. The full bin is turned into the empty bin and then the next week the process is done in reverse.

Amazingly, an active compost pile can heat up in the center to around 140 degrees. Composting will slow down over the colder winter months, but even then, you may see steam coming off the pile. Keep adding new ingredients, if possible, all winter long, even if the pile isn't turned. Then, come spring, the mixing and turning can start up again.

A great advantage of making your own compost is that you know exactly what ingredients have been added. For example, you know if the lawn clippings contain chemicals or not. This will help you regulate how "organic" your garden will stay.

ORGANIC FERTILIZER

Compost supplies undoubtedly the best form of organic fertilizer. Not only are nutrients added to

the soil, but the entire structure and texture of the soil is improved. The nutrients found in the leaves of large trees are particularly helpful in adding the trace amounts of nutrients needed for good plant growth. Those extensive roots wander deeply and widely to absorb nutrients for the growing tree. You get the benefit when we gather the fallen leaves for our composting process. If your neighborhood is not yet blessed with very large trees, go a gleaning come fall. I have a neighbor who is delighted when I come with my bags and tarps to "help" with the raking. Then, to make my presence even more appreciated, I haul off the leaves for my garden! (Double duty—helpful neighbor and compost builder.)

I do caution you to reconsider just taking bags of leaves that have been put out on the curb for garbage or recycle pick-up. Not everyone is considerate enough to keep unwanted garbage out of the bags seemingly filled with only leaves. It only takes one filled disposable diaper to make you a believer. Either help rake and bag yourself or make at least passing acquaintance with the folks from whom you get the bagged leaves.

To keep the composting process really moving along more quickly, not to mention giving your neighbors something to chuckle over, dump the leaves on your driveway and run over them several times with your lawnmower. This will reduce the bulk of the leaves from several bags to a few inches of leaf pieces. Not only does this take less space but it serves at least two other purposes. One is that large leaves tend to shuffle themselves into tight layers in the compost bin. These layers can eliminate air circulation and trap moisture, leading to rotting. You know what that means—wheeuuuuu! It will stink in there when you try to turn the pile. The stinking residue is slimy and yucky. That's definitely not compost.

Another purpose served is to speed up the composting process. The little microorganisms creating compost work more quickly on tiny pieces of raw material than great big leaves or stems. Or rinds or peels for that matter. It's kind of messy to run banana peels through the lawnmower, though.

There are also commercially available organic fertilizers on the market, which can be used to supplement or even stand instead of compost. Do remember though, compost does more for the soil than just add nutrients. The bagged or boxed products are merely specific nutrient supplements.

Organic fertilizers are much more available in garden centers and nurseries than they were fifteen years ago. I believe this has come to pass because gardeners, like you, have been learning about the benefits to the soil and plants from these products. Thanks to millions of gardeners just like you—especially like you newbies who haven't been trained in the way of chemical fertilizers—who have asked, pleaded, and searched for organic alternatives, we can all make different choices for our gardens.

UNDERSTANDING FERTILIZER

The percentage of the basic nutrients must be listed on every fertilizer bag. These numbers are identified by three numbers separated by hyphens: 10-10-10. The first number is the percentage of nitrogen in the fertilizer, and is often represented by the capital letter N. The middle number is the percentage of phosphorus and P is the symbol for that element. The final number is for potassium and the symbol

is K. These three major nutrients must be listed on every fertilizer container. These three elements are called the major nutrients and are referred to as the NPK portion of a fertilizer.

Nitrogen (N) is necessary for strong green leaves. A deficiency leaves plants weak, sometimes stunted, with pale green leaves. When nitrogen is added to the soil, it gives a boost to leaf production but can lead to fewer flowers and fruits because all the energy goes toward producing extra leaves. Ammonium sulfate gives a turbo boost to leaf production in lawns. This readily available fertilizer is very quickly dissolved after application and just as quickly absorbed by the little grass plants. You can nearly watch the grass growing right before your eyes! It results in a brilliant green lawn within three or four days. The unintended consequences include the need to mow *twice* a week or bring in two sheep to keep the lawn under control and an extended invitation to any passing insect that likes to devour grass. Also prompted by the extra lush succulent grass blades, lawn diseases are likely to show up in the lawn where you've never seen them before. That tender growth has little resistance to either diseases or insects.

Phosphorus (P) develops more root growth as well as better flower and fruit production. It is the root growth that is important to the lawn health. Longer, deeper, more numerous roots make for stronger healthier grass plants.

Plants need adequate Potassium (K) for general vigor and plant health and resistance. Many soils have sufficient potassium so a smaller number (percentage) of K on the label of a fertilizer is okay.

When all three of these major nutrients are combined in a fertilizer, regardless of their percentages, the fertilizer is said to be "a complete fertilizer." 10–10–10 is complete and equal. Packages listing 5–65–14 is unequal in portions but is still called a complete fertilizer. Plants also need other nutrients in smaller amounts than the major NPK. Some, like iron, are called *minor nutrients* and still others, like molybdenum, are called *trace elements*.

Organic matter is really the best long-term remedy for your soil. The addition of 3–4 inches of good compost dug into the top 7–8 inches of soil needs to take place before the lawn is first planted! The organic stuff (compost) needs to be decomposed down to good brown stuff, not fresh. Fresh means you can still recognize what it was, and it smells like exactly where it came from. You can buy it in bulk from many full service nurseries and garden centers.

Ammonium sulfate *is* a nitrogen source but it is detrimental to micro and macro life in the soil. Instead, add 2 inches of the organic material again next spring and fall and then the next spring and fall and the next . . . it will continue to break down in the soil year after year releasing all the nutrients, nitrogen included, that your soil and plants need.

It pleases me to no end to see that even the largest chemical companies are now producing an "organic line" of fertilizers, herbicides, and pesticides. Way to go, gardeners!

EARTHWORMS

A productive ally in the business of making good organic soil is the lowly earthworm. Worms can "work" or turn the soil several feet down by eating, burrowing, dropping castings (we're talking worm poop here), and working their way back to the sur-

Bonus Box: Earthworms are neither a him nor a her. They are hermaphrodites, that means they can make little worms with or without the benefit of a partner. They can, since they have both male and female reproductive parts, fertilize themselves or swap opposite pieces of their genetic makeup with any good-looking worm that wanders by.

Extra Bonus Box: Compost Tea can be easily brewed up to make your own liquid fertilizer. Pour 4 gallons of warm water into a bucket. Scoop 1 gallon of fresh, good compost into a panty-hose sack and tie the ends closed. Lower it down into the water and cover the bucket. Let the "tea" steep for about a week. Remove the pantyhose bag and water flowers and vegetables with the compost tea. Manure tea can be made and used the same way substituting well-cured manure for the compost.

face. How do you get the little wrigglers to come to your garden? Organic matter in the soil will help a lot. These naturally-occurring garden helpers are already in the soil, so there is no need to go buy earthworms. If you keep adding compost, they will come. And they reproduce prolifically when they get to your garden!

So, are you troubled by sandy soil that drains away your water faster than you can say "water bill"? Simply add organic matter.

Maybe you're plagued by slick, pull-the-boot-right-off-your-foot clay soil. Adding organic matter can improve that too.

There are several good sources for organic matter that comes bagged. This is a real boon to those with only *trunks*—not trucks. The quality of the bagged product is usually directly proportional to the cost per bag. The more expensive compost is usually the most nutritious. Beware of straight manure products. They are often high in salts, not completely composted, and can damage your plants. That stuff usually smells pretty rank, too. In fact, if you can tell by taking a whiff that it was once in a cow or horse or mink, and so on, it hasn't *really* been composted much at all.

Ordinarily, the bagged products won't say "organic matter" on the label. Instead, the bags may say "compost," "mulch," "humus," "soil conditioner," "manure," or even "fine bark." The more variety of products you add to the soil, the more nutrients will be present. Either mix different kinds of bagged material, or read the label to see how many different ingredients went into the bag.

Read the labels—some commercial bags will have a wide variety of organic matter already mixed together.

ORGANIC WEED CONTROL

Weeds are simply plants growing in places you don't want them to—plants that you consider undesirable, but insist on growing in your garden anyway and are hard to pull. But that is a personal bias! All gardens, even the most seemingly weed-free, contain weed seeds, some buried for decades just waiting to see the light of day to start growing. Others come to the garden by wind, water, animals, and even by soil amendments brought in to help gardens grow.

Nearly forty years ago my front and back garden were free from Field Bindweed (Wild Morning Glory or Vine from Hell). Then one day a little Cub Scout came to my door, all spiffy in his pressed blue shirt with bandana and little patches. The Den was having

a fundraiser—for fifteen dollars they would bring composted manure for my garden and even spread it around for me. Now, how can you turn down a Cub with cap in hand and grin on face. So a week later came a half dozen Cubs and a couple of adults with an entire pickup truck full of manure.

The manure was reasonably composted because I only caught an occasional whiff of barnyard aroma. And true to their word, they spread it over all of my front garden beds. Over the next couple of weeks I harvested rocks and mixed in the lovely organic amendment. It took just over a year for the first tiny tendril of destruction to appear—or so I remember. I also remember not paying much attention to those

> **Bonus Box:** Wearing surgical gloves when weeding keeps your hands clean and protected, yet allows you to easily feel the soil and the plants. Gloves also protect from any sprays used—no matter how organic and natural they may be.

initial little plants. From that tiny beginning came my endless Battle of the Bindweed. Yep, it's everywhere. And since I moved some of that lovely amended soil from my front flower beds to the vegetable garden, you guessed it, the vine pokes out from nearly all the growing beds in the backyard as well. You have been warned—against bindweed, not Cub Scouts!

When those weeds appear, the first impulse may be to wage chemical warfare, but, wait, there are other methods:

- **In the weed war, prevention is the first line of defense.** It's important to provide the healthiest conditions for growing desirable plants. Soil compaction, improper watering and diseases can trigger weed growth. A good deep, (3–4 inches at least) layer of mulch can prevent these problems as well as blocking the sunlight needed for weed seed germination.

- **Lay down a weed barrier.** Commercial landscape fabric is available and makes a great weed barrier in yard landscaping. Often it is covered with bark, mulch, or rocks making a somewhat permanent weed barrier. In the vegetable garden, plastic can be laid down around plants to block weeds. Hot-weather plants are ideally suited to this such as tomatoes, melons, and pumpkins. These are the veggies that thrive in extra warm soil. Only use this single layer, solid plastic sheet where you can remove and replace it easily. Sunlight causes the plastic to get brittle and break into pieces. Wet newspaper topped with grass clipping or straw is an excellent barrier that can be turned into the soil in the spring. Old carpet, turned nap side down, makes a great weed barrier for paths.

- **The most often used tool in the weed war is hand-to-hand combat**—just pulling those weeds out. This is best done when the soil is moist. The idea is to pull out as much of the root as possible.

- **Using a hoe or weeding tool in the garden will help keep the weed siege at bay.** Frequent use of these weapons will help you get them while they're young. Most weeds can just be turned under in the soil—but beware doing this with those such as Field Bindweed that easily sprout from even just a piece of the plant. And check carefully that the little invaders haven't already started to set seed.

- **Corn gluten meal can be used as a pre-emergent against weeds**— but only as a pre-emergent. After the root of a weed is established, corn gluten meal acts only as a fertilizer. This is great for lawns. It usually takes two to three years for corn gluten to become really effective—so apply once or twice a year and don't weaken or get discouraged.

- **Pour some boiling water on the offending weed.** For weeds isolated in driveways, cracks of sidewalks, or stairs, this method will effectively kill annoying weeds. Watch them shrivel and die within a short time. Just be careful not to get the hot water on yourself or any nearby desirable plant. Plain vinegar sprayed on little annual weeds in those same areas can be effective—I recommend you keep your tasty Balsamic vinegar for your salads and pasta and use plain old distilled vinegar for the weed spritzing.

- **A rather industrial strength, but effective way of weeding is to invest in a flame-weeder.** This nifty little gadget is a wand that hooks to a propane tank and a flame is directed at the weed. It doesn't burn the plant but rather the high heat destroys the cell structure of the weed and it dies. Only truly deadly to annual weeds, the instant gratification upon seeing dandelions, bindweed, and mallow shrivel and blacken has its own merits.

There are many additional weapons in the arsenal. Scuffle the little invaders off at the knees with a hoe. Get down and dig the dandelions with a long trusted, effective dandelion digger. Grow the thickest, healthiest lawn possible, and eliminate the areas of stress for your lawn.

Persistence is the key to successful weed control. Turn your back for a week, a month, or a season, and you'll soon find you are losing the war. Even a single day can turn the tide in a highly contested battle zone.

ORGANIC PEST CONTROL

A healthy garden discourages pests of the insect variety, but there is still nothing more frustrating than to find that little nibblers have sampled your garden goodies. Using some natural remedies from common ingredients found in the kitchen you can fend off many unwanted visitors.

Spend a few minutes every day in your yard and garden. Not only is it relaxing, but you can spot any potential problems right at the beginning and nip them in the bud! (No pun intended.) It may be that the saying "The best pest control is the gardener's shadow" comes from that "bud nipping" that happens when you visit your garden daily.

BIOLOGICAL CONTROLS

It is possible to control some pests with selective fatal diseases that only affect the pest you are aiming for—mostly. A common strain of bacteria (*Bacillus thuringiensis*) causes a fatal disease in the larvae of some insects. The common abbreviation for this tongue twister of a wee beastie is Bt. It will, in fact, kill the worms (caterpillars) that eat all the flowers on petunia and geranium plants. Because it is so specific in the organisms it infects, this disease will leave every other living thing without problems. The disease makes the caterpillar stop eating, and it soon dies. Treating tomato plants with the product *will* kill the huge green tomato hornworm but look closely before applying the liquid or powder (or as closely as your nerves will allow. The *thing* is often 4 to 5 inches long, as big around as your middle finger and has a black spine protruding from its back.)

If you see very teensy white specks that look like miniature grains of rice hooked to the top of even tinier little wire-looking threads, gird up your courage and let nature take its course. Those little grains are eggs of a beneficial insect—the Brachonid wasp—that will hatch and kill not only your hornworms but the ones in your neighbor's gardens as well.

There is a pest that causes damage in the garden by boring into the trunks of some fruit trees, those with pits, called stone fruit. While the larva is under the bark it destroys the living part of the tree that produces the conductive tissue in the tree. This is the Greater Peach Tree borer, and it is the larva of this black and white moth that does the damage. Treatment to prevent damage to the trunk of stone fruit trees can include painting the trunk of the tree with a Bt solution. The solution should be applied around the first week of July, August, and again in September. These dates roughly correspond with the time of egg-laying of the female moth. You need only treat the lower 12 to 15 inches of the trunk extended to just a little below the soil line. Move the soil back from the trunk while painting on the solution and then just push the soil back against the trunk. This should be done at least three times, three to five days apart at the beginning of the three months.

Organic or botanical pesticides are often mistaken for something totally harmless to you and the environment. Not so! Just because the source is not a man-made chemical doesn't mean it is without consequences when used. READ THE LABEL every time you use the product.

> **Bonus Box:** Your local county extension office is a great resource and can help identify and solve garden problems that may arise. Often they hold regular diagnostic clinics where you can get answers and solutions to any plant problems you may have difficulty diagnosing on your own.

IN SUMMARY

Organic landscapes may not be as picture-perfect as those where chemical warfare has been waged. There may be a few more weeds or insect pests, most of which are benign and aren't causing any problems at all. Try not to begrudge a bite or two of this or that—remember the Bad Guy Bugs are what keep the Good Guy Bugs fed! We don't want to starve out our best little helpers, now do we?

Shared harvest and blemishes notwithstanding, the benefits far outweigh the disadvantages. The soil in an organic garden becomes richer and more nutrient-laden every season. Little bare feet can run across the lawn with no worry of chemical contamination. Vegetables picked and eaten from the garden are healthy and safe—and taste great. It's safer and more inviting to spend some quality summer hours lying on the lawn just watching the clouds go by! In other words, organic just feels right!

NATURAL REMEDIES TO CURE PLANT DISEASES

REMEDY	PROBLEMS
2 non-coated aspirin, dissolved in 1 quart water, sprayed on foliage.	Fights mildew and blackspot
Milk and Water Spray 1 part milk with 5 to 9 parts water	Control of powdery mildew
Good watering practices— water evenly and regularly.	Prevention of many problems such as blossom end rot in tomatoes.
Crop Rotation	Rotation of crops from year to year will prevent many disease problems before they get started.

NATURAL REMEDIES TO COMMON PROBLEMS

REMEDY	PROBLEM
Shaking Branches	Shoos away the flying variety of insects—simple but a good first step.
Strong Stream of Water	Washes off aphids and mites. Be sure to get the underside of leaves as well.
Garlic Spray • Puree several garlic cloves in a little bit of water. • A few tablespoons of liquid soap—not detergent. • Add to 1 gallon of water. • For a more potent spray, add some cayenne pepper and onions. • Let steep in the water. • Strain (so the sprayer doesn't get clogged) and spray as needed.	Great pesticide as well as fungicide. The sulfur compounds in the garlic help prevent fungal diseases such as tomato blight, downy mildew, and cucumber rust. Also gets rids of cabbage worms, wireworms, ants, whiteflies, aphids, slugs, cutworms, and caterpillars.
Dishwater • Pour dishwater in a watering can and recycle it onto your plants. • For the same result, mix 3–5 tablespoons of mild dishwashing soap in one gallon of water. Soft water is better than hard water. • Apply in the cool mornings	Controls soft-bodied insects such as aphids, thrips, and mites. This and insecticidal soap must come in contact with the insect to take effect. After it dries on the plant, it does not work.
Insecticidal Soap • Commercial product • Stronger than above • All sprays work better with a few drops of soap added. It helps the sprays stick to the plants and the insects.	Controls many of the insects listed above plus whiteflies and the immature stage of mealy bug and scale insect.
Boiling Water	Poured on an ant bed, the problem will soon be solved. Be careful not to get the hot water on any plants or grass.

REMEDY	PROBLEM
Citrus Peel Spray • Peel from one orange • 2 cups hot water • Let steep for 24 hours • Strain out the peels • Add 3–4 drops of dishwashing soap • Spray	Ants and other insects react to the natural pesticides found in citrus peelings.
Diatomaceous Earth • can be found at garden centers or nurseries	Sprinkling diatomaceous earth where there is an insect problem will control ants, earwigs, slugs, snails, aphids. Excellent around areas where ants enter the house and in the house as well.
Bucket of soapy water	Handpick off any unwanted insects or use kitchen tongs to touch the undesirables. Drop them in the bucket of soapy water and later dispose.
Grits	Sprinkling grits will solve an ant problem. The ants eat the grits, the grits expand and . . . well, you get the picture.
Row Cover • Commercial product	Covering plants with row cover will keep out unwanted insects. An example would be to cover cabbages before the cabbage moth lays eggs and the eggs hatch into little munching caterpillars.
Mineral Oil and Clothespin	To prevent corn earworms, spray or drop 12–20 drops of mineral oil on the tassels of an ear of corn. (Makes husking the ear of corn easier too!) Also, a clothespin can be used to close off the tip of the ear of corn.
Beneficial Insects • ladybugs • praying mantis	Use of natural remedies for harmful insects will keep the beneficial insects alive and well.

REMEDY	PROBLEM
Newspaper	Earwigs love to hide in wet, rolled-up newspaper. Place where there is a problem and discard each morning in a plastic bag or shake into a bucket of soapy water.
Red Pepper Spray • 1 gallon water • 6 tablespoons liquid soap • 3 tablespoons red pepper • Mix and let sit for 2 or 3 days. • Spray	Use to protect all plants in the cabbage family—cabbage, cauliflower, broccoli, brussels sprouts, and kale
Copper Strips	If using raised garden boxes, place copper strips around the outer edge of the box to keep away slugs.
Orange and Grapefruit rinds	Orange and grapefruit rinds will attract both slugs and snails. Use the half rind and prop it up with a little pebble or stick, one side just a little way off the ground. Next morning dump the critters into a bag with or without the peel since it can be used again, then tie off the bag and put it into the garbage.
Yeasty beverage • cheap, bitter beer or yeast and a little sugar in water	Bury a shallow dish, like a pie tin, up to the rim in an area near the snail's daytime hideaway. Fill the dish with the liquid. In they go and drown. Dump the snail soup and repeat the next night.

Organic Animal Control

NATURAL REMEDIES TO KEEP CRITTERS AWAY

REMEDY	PROBLEMS	REMEDY	PROBLEMS
Cayenne Pepper, sprinkled on wet vegetables leaves (spray first with water)	Keep away rabbits	Fences	Always a good idea to keep large animals from the garden, but it takes an eight-foot fence to keep out deer.
Plastic Utensils	Keeps cats away. Yes, really! Stick plastic forks, knives, or spoons in an area that has been newly planted with seed. This will keep cats from using it as a litter box until the seeds sprout and the plants grow.	Protective cages	Individual cages made from chicken wire can be placed over garden boxes or sections of a garden to protect from animals.
Rotten egg, garlic mixture, spoiled fish (or any combination of the above)	Deer don't like really bad smells. A mixture like this will keep deer away—may also work on unwanted visitors as well.	Scarecrows, Mylar streamers, wind chimes	A combination of these scare off birds for a short time. Move and change the display regularly so that the birds don't get used to it.
Soap from hotels	Deer are repelled by the smell of *strong* soap. Hang soap from trees, or nail to stakes or fence posts.	Flour and cayenne pepper. 1 cup flour to 2 tablespoons cayenne.	Sprinkle on cabbage to keep out the cabbage worm. The flour gets the cabbage worm and the cayenne pepper takes care of other pests.
Human or animal hair	Deer stay away from the smell of human or animal hair—the longer and more unwashed the better. Sprinkle it around the garden or hang in little mesh bags about three feet off the ground. Must be refreshed about once a month, more often if it rains or snows.	Neem Oil – Commercial 2 tablespoons per gallon of water. Mix frequently as you spray. Completely wet tops and undersides of leaves.	Many uses—insecticide, miticide and fungicide. Controls various diseases as well as insects and mites. Use on vegetables, fruit trees, and ornamentals.
Wire mesh	To keep burrowing animals from popping up in your garden and if you are using garden boxes, attach fine wire mesh to the bottom of the boxes before filling with soil. Keeps kitties from using garden areas as a litter box when laid flat on the ground and covered with a very light layer of mulch		

THIS 'N THAT 'N ZONES 'N CHARTS

TOOLS

Having the right tools on hand helps get a gardener off on the right foot, or hand, as it were. Purchase sturdy tools that will serve you well for a long time to come. One exception to this rule is to buy several inexpensive trowels, especially if you have one or more children under the age of eight who "really need the little shovel." This is a point in favor of the *many-for-the-price-of-one* approach, rather than the *start-with-quality-because-it-lasts* buying of tools. However, if you want the tool to stay by your side through years of gardening, stick with quality instead of quantity.

BASIC "GARDEN STARTING" TOOLS:

- **Hoe:** So many kinds! One to cut off weeds at ground level and one to dig furrows—some types are better for certain chores—try an oscillating (Hula) hoe for surface weeding and a heart shaped hoe for furrows.

- **Hose:** A good, long garden hose that doesn't kink along with an adjustable-stream nozzle for watering is a must for gardeners. Start with a medium grade—not the cheapest possible. Kinks will drive you krazy!

- **Rake:** Leaf rake made of bamboo, plastic, or metal. Not essential until you have trees large enough to drop leaves or you live downwind from neighbors with large trees. Garden rake with metal tines (the forky part) and wood or plastic handle. Best for leveling soil, sand or small rocks.

- **Shovel:** Regular old wooden handle, metal scoop; a smaller size called Floral Shovel is handy for digging in tight spaces and easier on the back because it holds a smaller amount of soil in each scoop. Not to be used for prying up rocks unless you want a broken handle for something else.

- **Trowel:** "Hand shovel" used for planting flowers and veggies. Some are very inexpensive—they are the kind for starting a garden, especially if young children are your helpers. Trowels disappear almost as quickly as pencils, combs, and single socks.

- **Weed Digger:** A sharp tool with a long forked shaft used to penetrate the soil and remove the weed—root and all. Also called a "dandelion digger."

SHOPPING

Elsewhere in this book is a section extolling the virtues of catalog and online purchases. I think it's a good idea to use those sources to create a list of plants and tools you would love to own. But buy from the  out-of-state businesses only if there is an exotic, super-specific tool or plant that just can't be found in your neck of the woods. For most purchases, take that list with you to a locally owned nursery or garden center and do your buying at the businesses near you. Ask a nursery professional for their opinion. Just because blueberries are your family's favorite fruit doesn't mean they will grow well in your area.

Local folks can direct you to varieties that will do best in your garden. They can explain why a Silver Maple may be gorgeous but will give you continual headaches if you live along the Wasatch Front in

> **Extra Bonus Box:** You'll meet the nicest people at plant sales. If you look overwhelmed and puzzled while trying to choose the best of the fifteen basil varieties, someone will usually step over to explain the virtues of Sweet Dani Basil versus Thai Basil and a new friendship is made.

Utah. The alkaline soil and lack of humidity just won't let that tree grow well, especially if you have clay soil. Try a trip to Pittsburgh if you want to see a gorgeous, strong Silver Maple. You can avoid the pitfalls of plants that grow well in the shade if you live in Texas but need more sun in Maine. And the nursery folks can show you where to find the lime (short for limestone, not the little green fruit essential for good fresh guacamole) for gardens in Oregon

> **High on a Mountain Tip:** Most high mountain valleys in the intermountain west are Zone 4 sometimes even dipping to a Zone 3.

but will keep you from trying to buy the lime to dig into your gardens in Colorado.

Once you get the feel for what you would like to try in your garden, or even just an inkling of what would be fun, visit a local plant sale. These sales can be as small as a fundraiser for a neighborhood elementary school or as elaborate as the annual fundraiser for your nearest botanical garden. On whatever scale, these sales focus on selling what grows well in your garden's climate.

ZONES

On most plant tags in tiny print, there is a designation showing which Zone the plant will grow, which is all fine and good except where do you find *what* Zone you are living in and more importantly, what *is* a Zone?

At some point in every gardener's life, they will fall in love with some plant just because they love the plant! Maybe it is the creamy white of the gardenia blossom; maybe its the impressive huge flowers of a Saucer magnolia; or it certainly could be the heavenly fragrance and fruit of an orange tree. Some get taken by the lovely spring flowers of a lilac, or the fruit and fall color of a blueberry bush or the gorgeous fanlike leaves of a palm tree.

When you are so smitten, you start looking around to find who is already growing your newfound love. Hmmmm—nary a one to be seen. Now, how can that be? How can gardeners on your street, in your town, or city be unaware of how spectacular this plant would be in their garden? So you head to your local nursery or garden center to solve the mystery of the unplanted beauty.

If you chance upon a gentle soul with years of gardening experience, they will smile kindly and explain, "In this Zone we can't grow that plant." A younger, less restrained employee may burst out with an embarrassing, "You want to grow *that* HERE? You're kidding, right?" Both have the information you wanted, or rather, didn't want to know. Because of elevation or summer heat or winter cold or the wrong soil or lack (or excess) of humidity or length of growing season—or a nasty combination of two or more of the above conditions—it is futile to try growing your beloved plant.

The Department of Agriculture puts together a map of the various regions of the United States with divided and color-coded areas that have approximately the same low temperatures during the winter. Plant zones range from 1 (plants that will tolerate temperatures minus 50° F) to 11 (plants that will only tolerate temperatures 40° F and above). Other organizations like ArborDay.org put together similar maps (see below). Calculated to help gardeners keep from freezing the knees off of plants that couldn't live in temperatures that dipped below, oh say 40 degrees, the Zone tolerance was then printed on plant tags.

Mighty fine idea! Except for a few hitches that developed in this "git along":

- These Zones only consider winter cold temperatures with nothing said about blistering summer heat.

- There is no mention of tolerance for high or low humidity.

- The need for a specific soil alkalinity or acidity isn't mentioned.

- The tags never explain if Zone 4 is warmer than Zone 6—it is assumed that everyone who buys a plant with a tag already knows this.

PLANT HARDINESS ZONE MAP

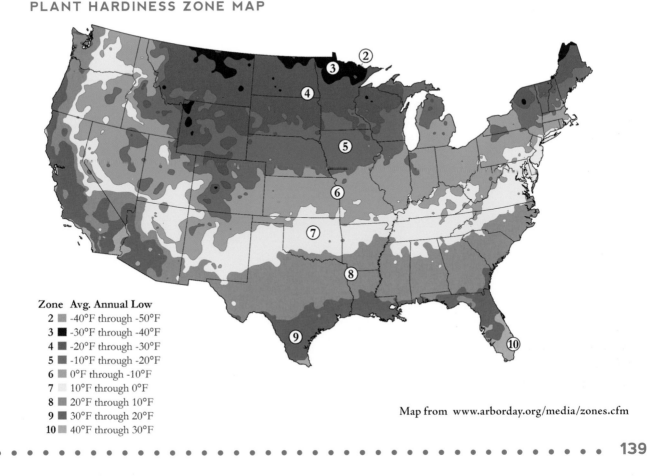

Zone Avg. Annual Low
2 -40°F through -50°F
3 -30°F through -40°F
4 -20°F through -30°F
5 -10°F through -20°F
6 0°F through -10°F
7 10°F through 0°F
8 20°F through 10°F
9 30°F through 20°F
10 40°F through 30°F

Map from www.arborday.org/media/zones.cfm

- If a plant is listed as Zone 4 (pretty cold weather) in the northeast part of the country, will it still grow in Zone 7? Will it make it through a winter or summer way down in the southern states?

Then to add to confusion—there are other designations of Zones chosen by other garden entities that don't match up at all with the USDA map and Zones. And there is still another Zone map designed to indicate how hot the summers get in a given area. Some plant tags say in small print that "this is a perennial" but in even tinier print it's listed as Zone 9. Well, partner, Zone 9 never sees so much as a frost, let alone a single snowflake. One winter in an intermountain garden and that little perennial shows itself to be a very expensive annual!

Here is an example of a Zone designation, sort of. Sort of because there are exceptions and differences of opinions:

Salt Lake City, Utah is Zone 5-ish. Most Zone 4 plants do well and more and more varieties that are listed as Zone 6 grow well here, thank you very much. Rarely can we stretch to safely grow plants from Zone 7, but that doesn't keep some of us from trying!

High on a Mountain Tip: Choose plants carefully and make sure they are suited to your zone. It is easy to fall to the temptation of owning a beautiful perennial in a catalog or nursery, only to buy it, plant it, and discover it doesn't winter over in your zone.

PLANTING CHART

One of the most frequently asked questions is when to plant what. A lot of variables are involved in that answer, but hopefully this chart will simplify some of that. Don't forget—the weather can change this time schedule from year to year so these are "abouts."

TYPE	PLANTS	PLANTING TIME	COMMENTS
Hardy Plants	Asparagus, Broccoli, Cabbage, Onions, Peas, Spinach, Radish, Rhubarb	Mid-March-ish in Zone 5	Plant as soon as you can work the soil. This goes for Zones 3 and 4 as well.
Half-Hardy Plants	All of the above, plus: Beets, Carrots, Cauliflower, Lettuce, Potatoes, Swiss Chard	Toward the end of March in Zone 5	Depends on if the snow has melted in Zones 3 and 4.
Tender Plants	Beans, Corn, Cucumbers, Summer Squash	Mid to end of May	Or about when apple blossoms first appear. Zones 3 and 4 need to be prepared with protection from frosts.
Very Tender Plants	Cantaloupe, Peppers, Winter Squash, Tomatoes, other melons	End of May to first part of June	Plant when the soil is warm. Again, cover up if in a colder Zone.

In my fifty years of paying attention to plants and especially their flowers, I can tell you that the growing season here has lengthened and moderated. Plants that could be counted on to provide flowers for Memorial Day now blossom nearly two weeks earlier leaving little to pick for bouquets to decorate the graves. This shift in season has also increased the number of plants we can now plant with increasing confidence that they will make it through our winter.

To determine what Zone your garden is in, you can consult a map, or better still, contact a local Master Gardener or extension office. They can give you a Zone number and also the exceptions and cautions.

FROST MAP

The last frost date for an area is the last day in the spring that it's likely you'll have a frost. It's important to recognize that the actual date of the last frost is different every year. It can be much earlier than the average or much later. This is especially important to note because tender plants can be killed in one night by a frost. For hardier plants, the average last frost date is more of an indicator of general growing conditions than a danger sign.

Microclimates play an important role in frost dates. Features like hills or water can significantly affect temperatures. There could possibly be a different actual last frost date just a few houses away.

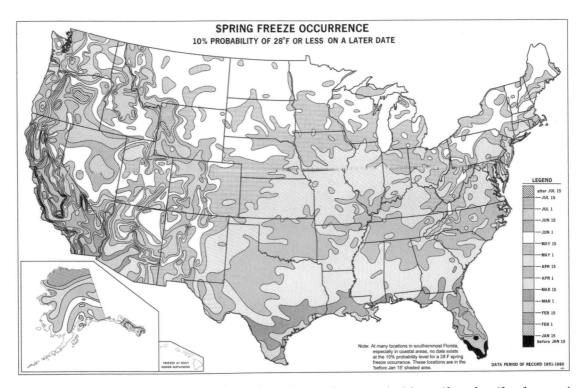

Map from the NOAA Satelite and Information Service, http://www.ncdc.noaa.gov/oa/climate/freezefrost/frostfreemaps.html

Glossary of Terms

Annual
Plants that complete the cycle from "seed to plant to flower and back to seed" in one growing season.

Backfill
To refill a trench or other excavation with the soil dug out of it.

Bark
From trees! Can be shredded, ground, chopped into chunks, small to large, mixed or partially composted.

Biennial
Lives for two years. Produces plant the first year and blossoms and seeds the second year. Often reseeds itself.

Branch collar
The swollen area of trunk tissue that forms around the base of a branch.

Broadleaf evergreen
Shrubs or trees that keep their leaves through the winter, but the leaves are not needle-like.

Central leader
The main trunk of the tree.

Compost
Partially finished product of the composting cycle—might be from manure, leaves, wood chips, weeds, kitchen scraps, vegetable peelings, fruit rinds, and so on. Mostly unrecognizable pieces.

Cotyledon
A leaf of the embryo of a seed plant, which upon germination either remains in the seed or emerges, enlarges, and becomes green. Also called seed leaf.

Cutting garden
Flowers grown in an area specifically to cut and put in a bouquet.

Deciduous
Plants that lose their leaves during the cold season and grow new ones in the growing season.

Dirt
Residue left on your car after a particularly short summer rain shower. Dirt is what accumulates in the corner of the garage or is tracked into the house on your feet. Dirt is what often masquerades as soil around a newly built home (especially if the house is the last one to be built in the neighborhood).

Dormant season
Time when plants are not actively growing.

Dwarf tree
Growth is from 6 to 20 feet tall, depending on the kind of tree.

Evergreen
Plants that maintain their green leaves year round.

Flush of blooms
Period of time when the majority of the flowers on a plant are blooming at the same time.

Fruit
The structure of the plant containing or associated with the seed or seeds.

Fruits (not from trees)
Small fruit: grapes, berries, currants.

Green Bin
Recycle container made available by some municipalities.

Growing Soil
(Verb) To create topsoil the old-fashioned way—one shovelful at a time. The never-ceasing struggle for truth, justice, and perfect garden loam. It's a continuous attempt by gardeners to thwart the natural tendency of soil to revert to dirt. Growing soil includes making consistent additions of organic matter to all existing garden areas. (Noun) The good stuff. Natural, homegrown, or artificial—into which your plants sink their roots.

Harden Off
A period of time young plants and seedlings are cared for before planting in the garden. This is done by setting the seedlings outside for a few hours in a sheltered location, leaving them out a little longer each day until they can stay out all day and all night. A week or two of doing this should acclimate them so they'll grow and flourish when transplanted.

Heading back
A branch or shoot is shortened. Older wood is headed back to an outward growing smaller branch. Heading back encourages lateral growth or branching.

Herbaceous
A plant without any woody tissue.

Humus
The final stage of the composting process. The material that is richest in nutrients. It consists of dark brown, uniform particles that don't resemble the beginning material that was composted.

Lime
Short for limestone, used to raise soil pH making the soil more alkaline.

Lug
(Verb) To carry an awkward or heavy object, or (Noun) a box for fruit and vegetables of specific size.

Manure
Backend product of living creatures: cows, horses, chickens, bats, earthworms, etc. Guano=Bat poop. Worm poop=Castings.

Microclimate
A microclimate is the climate of a small area that is different from the area around it. Microclimate can be modified by buildings, walls, low areas, other plants, and so forth.

Mulch
A generic term for something used on top of the soil to retain moisture, inhibit weeds, and modify soil temperature; may or may not be organic.

Ornamentals
A plant grown for beauty rather than for food.

Overseed
To add grass seed to an existing sparse lawn to create a thicker healthier lawn or to fill in the spaces left after power raking.

Pasty
Pa (as in *hat*) **sty;** not to be confused with **Pa** (as in *ape*)**sty.**
The traditional Cornish pasty is a turnover filled with diced meat, sliced potato and onion, and baked.

Perennial
That plant, if planted in your father's garden, would have come back year after year. The return rate in *your* garden is inversely proportional to the money spent on the plant: 4 for $10 plants return for many years, a $60 specialty Peony croaks the first winter.

Saffron crocus
Small, lavender fall-blooming flower; source of the spice saffron.

Scaffold branch
Five to eight main (and largest) branches on a fruit tree. Should have crotches at a wide angle.

Soil Conditioner
Any one or a mixture of some of the organic material dug into the soil. Also called soil amendment—check the fine print on the label to determine what is *really* in the bag.

Standard tree
One that reaches full size; for apples that is 30–40 feet tall; Blue spruce is 60+ feet tall and 25–30 feet across.

Starts
Small, young plants.

Succession Planting
Spacing time of the planting of vegetables to ensure a continuous harvest rather than having the entire crop ready all at once.

Tamp
To pack or push something down, especially by tapping it repeatedly.

Thinning out
Entire shoots or branches are removed back to a lateral branch.

Top Dressing
Material, usually organic, used in a ½ to 1-inch layer to make garden beds look neat and tidy. Like when company is coming or a reception is going to be held in your backyard.

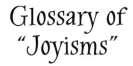

Glossary of "Joyisms"

Bejeebers
Most every little part.

Clank
Sound of first contact between shovel and rock of any size

First-ish
Means round about, near to, give or take a couple of whatever unit of measure you are referring to.

Fooey
Means, "I don't believe that for a minute."

Gardenees
All plants, great and small, in your garden—or even in the cracks in your sidewalk, for that matter.

Okey Dokey
"Roll up your sleeves; we're ready to tackle another project." To be said or read, with emphasis on the **DOK**ey!

Nobbley
Having extra knobs rather than a single shape.

Propper-Upper
A device used to keep something from falling down.

Righty Dighty
"Agreed! Right on! That's for sure."

Scritch
A horrible sound indicating that a shovel has not only contacted and slid down a rock of large but yet-to-be determined size, but has yet to find the bottom of said rock.

Sticky-outy
With loose ends, not tightly wound or pressed together

Squinching
Tightening of the facial muscles into a grimace.

Thwapped
Struck with sudden and surprising force.

Weed
A plant growing in the wrong place that is hard to pull.

Willey Nilley
A little here, a little there, no rhyme nor reason

Joy and Karen's Favorite Books and Resources

BOOKS

Trowel & Error
By Sharon Lovejoy
Workman Publishing Company
www.workman.com

Time Life How-To Landscaping Projects
Time-Life Books

Gardening Basics for Dummies
By Steven A. Frowine
Wiley Publishing Inc.
www.wiley.com

Better Homes and Gardens New Complete Guide to Gardening
By Susan A. Roth
Meredith Group

Sunset Garden Book—Western Edition

All New Square Foot Gardening
By Mel Bartholomew
Cool Springs Press

THREE OTHER INTERESTING BOOKS TO CONSIDER

The Earth Moved
By Amy Stewart

The Gardener's Bed-Book
By Richardson Wright

The Man Who Planted Trees
By Jean Giono

MAGAZINES

Organic Gardening
33 East Minor St.
Emmaus, PA 18098
Phone: (610) 967-5171
www.organicgardening.com
(If you aren't already acquainted with this one, I strongly recommend you buy at least one issue and read it cover to cover, every page)

Country Gardens
1716 Locust St.
Des Moines, IA 50309-3023
www.BHG.com/countrygardens

Fine Gardening
The Taunton Press
63 South Main St.
P.O. Box 5506
Newtown, CT 06470-5506
Phone: (800) 888-8286
support@customerservice.taunton.com
www.finegardening.com

WEBSITES

For information about Joy in the Garden
www.570knrs.com, keyword: Joy
www.joyinthegarden.com

For information on Karen's speaking schedule
See Karen's page at www.joyinthegarden.com

CATALOGS

Burpee Gardens
300 Park Avenue
Warminster, PA 18974
Phone: (800) 888-1447
Fax: (800) 487-5530
custserv@burpee.com
www.burpee.com
Catalog request via "snail-mail":
032763 Burpee Building
Warminster, PA 18974
Flower and vegetable seeds, plants, some shrubs, vines, roses, hedges., many hybrids. Some supplies.

Gardens Alive!
5100 Schenley Place
Lawrenceburg, IN 47025
Phone: (812) 537-8650
Fax: (812) 537-5108
gardenhelp@gardens-alive.co
www.gardens-alive.com
Organic and environmentally friendly everything! Fertilizers, pesticides including Escar-go, bird food, garden tools, and decorations.

High Country Gardens
2902 Rufina Street
Santa Fe, NM 87505-2929
Phone: (800) 925-9837
Fax: (800) 925-0097
www.highcountrygardens.com
Water-wise plants, perennials, cacti, succulents, shrubs, grasses, herbs.

Nichols Garden Nursery
1190 North Pacific Highway NE
Albany OR 97321-4580
Phone: (866) 408-4850
Fax: (800) 231-5306
www.nicholsgardennursery.com
Core sponsor of safe seed initiative (against genetically engineered plants or seeds), herb and rare seeds, herb plants, vegetable seeds, edible flower seeds, herb teas, essential oils, books, recipes.

Stark Bro's
Hwy 54 West
Louisiana, MO 63353
Phone: (573) 754-5111
Fax: (573) 754-3701
www.starkbros.com
Many original hybrid fruit trees, small fruits, ornamental trees, as well as familiar varieties.

Totally Tomatoes
PO Box 1626
Augusta, GA 30903-1626
Phone: (803) 663-0217
Fax: (888) 477-7333
www.totallytomato.com
Novelty tomatoes, new varieties, many heirloom varieties, some peppers and cucumbers.

Wayside Gardens
1 Garden Lane
Hodges, SC 29695-0001
Phone: (800) 845-1124
Fax: (800) 457-9712
info@waysidegardens.com

www.waysidegardens.com
Perennial plants, old roses, shrubs of all kinds, evergreens, hostas, many new introductions.

Johnny's Selected Seeds
955 Benton Avenue,
Winslow, ME 04901
Phone: (877) 564-6697
Fax: (800) 738-6314
www.johnnyseeds.com
Seeds, supplies, and information. Many organically grown varieties. Excellent website.

OTHER RESOURCES

Master Gardener Associations
Classes, activities, and opportunities to rub shoulders, or shovels, with other gardeners while learning more about hands-on gardening in your local area.

County Extension Office
Visit or call your local extension office to obtain information specific to your area. Classes and activities held; pamphlets; books; diagnostic clinics. The Cooperative Extension System is a nationwide, non-credit educational network. Each U.S. state and territory has a state office at its land-grant university and a network of local or regional offices. These offices are staffed by one or more experts. To locate the office nearest you, visit www.csrees.usda.gov/Extension/index.

Botanical Gardens
Visit local botanical gardens to see the plants that do well in your area. A botanical garden's charge is to provide education, seminars, classes, and other activities, which are held regularly.

Arboretum
An excellent place to view a wide variety of trees and shrubs before deciding what you want in your own yard. Often located within a botanical garden.

Locally Owned Nurseries and Garden Centers
These nurseries and garden centers give more personalized customer service and have employees that know the plants that are appropriate and available for your area.

Local Public and Private Gardens
Great places to get ideas and suggestions from local gardeners.

Local Garden Tours
Sponsored by various groups. Both professional gardening and non-profit clubs and associations host a wide variety of garden tours through both public and private gardens.

Local Community Gardens
Interesting to visit and can be downright quirky and fun. For instance, the International Peace Gardens and Gilgal Garden in Salt Lake City, Utah are two of the best-kept secrets in that community! Nearly every town and city has one or more gardens that can become your favorite garden haunt and refuge, once you find them.